To

....

From

....

Date

....

GLENN HASCALL

MAN OF STRENGTH

100 DEVOTIONS *for*
a LIFE OF POWER

BARBOUR
PUBLISHING

© 2023 by Barbour Publishing, Inc.

ISBN 978-1-63609-638-4

Adobe Digital Edition (.epub) 978-1-63609-766-4

Published by Barbour Publishing, Inc., 1810 Barbour Drive, Uhrichsville, Ohio 44683, www.barbourbooks.com

Our mission is to inspire the world with the life-changing message of the Bible.

Member of the
Evangelical Christian
Publishers Association

Printed in China.

**Men, set a powerful example for the world.
Be the person God wants you to be
with *Man of Strength* devotions.**

Masculinity has come under fire in recent years, but
the world needs Christian men like never before. *Man
of Strength: 100 Devotions for a Life of Power* celebrates
men, the ones who rely on God for His strength, exercise
their spiritual muscles each day, and deny themselves the
thoughts and actions that create weakness in a guy.

Each entry encourages you to "be the man"—the
man who

- admits his weakness
- celebrates God's strength
- lets God judge
- never gives up

among dozens of other bold, God-honoring behaviors.

You'll be challenged and encouraged to fill your God-
given role in your home, your workplace, your community,
and your world.

BE THE MAN
WHO LIVES BEYOND
THE CRUEL

Their lives became full of every kind of wickedness, sin, greed, hate, envy, murder, quarreling, deception, malicious behavior, and gossip.

ROMANS 1:29 NLT

You could take some time right now to set this book down and read the latest news instead. You could dwell on the tragedies and determine that the state of the world is cruel, disheartening and, well, awful.

You could do these things. . .but why would you? After all, the news cycle is pretty predictable. It's just a summary of Romans 1:29—all the stuff that no one wants to see, just in a new package each day.

The more time you spend with this kind of news to the exclusion of God's good news, the more strength is leached from your internal storehouse. When the bad news gets a higher spot on your priority list than the Bible's encouraging words, you'll miss the joyful infusion that only God can give.

You could take a spiritual bath in cruelty, or you could be restored, replenished, and refreshed by good news, which leads to new strength. Even when it seems like the latest inhumanity demands your full attention, you have the choice to live beyond the cruel. To reach beyond wickedness. To survive without the gossip. The choice is simple. . .but often overlooked.

God's Word doesn't pass on faulty intel. It never requires a retraction or alteration. So when your cruel culture seems more menacing than inviting, make the better choice! God's strength is always available—and it's the only way to get by in a Romans 1:29 world.

How can news suppress your inner strength?
Why can God's Word have the opposite effect?

BE THE MAN
WHO ADMITS WEAKNESS

"Pardon me, my lord," Gideon replied, "but how can I save Israel? My clan is the weakest in Manasseh, and I am the least in my family."

JUDGES 6:15 NIV

When Gideon explained to God that he was the weakest in an already weak family, God essentially told him, "I know. But you don't need your strength when you have Mine!"

God's messenger angels addressed Gideon as a "mighty warrior." That's why Gideon insisted that there must've been a mistake. But God doesn't make mistakes. Gideon would need to come to terms with the fact that his personal self-assessment was no longer the truth.

Judges 6–7 goes on to describe what God did with this "weak" man. When Gideon raised thirty-two thousand soldiers to defeat a national enemy, God said that this was too many. So He started thinning the pack. If any soldier was afraid, God gave him permission to leave.

Ten thousand remained. But to God, this was *still*

too many. If Gideon went to war with ten thousand men, people might overlook the fact that God was the true deliverer.

In the end, only three hundred men remained—an army with zero chance for success unless God stepped in. And He did.

By admitting weakness, Gideon made a great decision. By avoiding the false idea that God helps those who help themselves, he became eligible for God's assistance.

The strength you need won't just bubble up from some internal artesian well. True strength comes solely from God. Stop looking for it elsewhere.

Why is it important for God to display His strength in your weakness? How can you let God know He is welcome to work through you?

BE THE MAN
WHO DOESN'T FEAR

Fear thou not; for I am with thee: be not dismayed; for I am thy God: I will strengthen thee; yea, I will help thee; yea, I will uphold thee with the right hand of my righteousness.

ISAIAH 41:10 KJV

Use your phone's calendar function to remind you. Leave a note on the fridge. Tie a string around your finger. Okay, ready? Take a deep breath and write this down:

THERE'S NO NEED TO BE AFRAID—
GOD IS WITH YOU RIGHT NOW.

Every day of your life, God is there to help. So at each moment, you have a choice between two pursuits: Do you worry yourself into weakness or turn to God for strength?

Some people make a full-time job out of peddling fear, and they are exceptional salesmen. You'll find anxiety for sale in advertising, the news, and even coffee shop conversations. There will always be something to be concerned about. Pretty soon, you'll find it easy to take up the salesman mantle yourself. But every time an unexpecting customer accepts a worry you know that person doesn't need, it'll only amplify your own.

God hates worry, and it's easy to see why. If you worry even after God has promised to be with you, this implies you've either missed His message or you're still struggling to trust Him.

You can be a man who embraces God's strength. . .but this means rejecting worry in favor of believing God is in control. Remember: He gives you strength, He stays with you, and His help is always on call.

When is the right time to worry? Do you find it hard to believe that God sees your choice to be anxious as an invitation to personal chaos?

BE THE MAN
WHO BREAKS UP
WITH PHOBIA

So you have not received a spirit that makes you fearful slaves. Instead, you received God's Spirit when he adopted you as his own children. Now we call him, "Abba, Father."

ROMANS 8:15 NLT

Did you know there are around four hundred named phobias? Even the ones that don't have a name are covered by an umbrella term. That word is *panophobia*—the fear of everything.

Fear comes in three main categories: social, specific, and crowds. You can be afraid to speak in public. You can be afraid of clowns. You can be afraid of people who are popular.

Some fears affect only a small number of people. For instance, *arachibutyrophobia* is the fear of peanut butter sticking to the roof of your mouth, and *xanthophobia* is the fear of the color yellow. You may think it's funny that someone could be afraid of either, but for someone who has these fears, it's no laughing matter.

Fear makes you weak. It keeps you from making positive decisions. It causes you to retreat before you can even choose to move forward. It locks you in a place of danger instead of leading you to safety.

But God sympathizes with us. That's why He made a habit of telling His people that fear is unnecessary. The choice to believe Him is yours—and He wants you to make it. To make positive decisions, move forward, and seek help.

A man of strength breaks up with fear and refuses to treat it like an old flame. There's no good reason to re-engage with the fear that made you ineffective. God has called you to a life of adventure—are you ready to receive His strength?

Why does God want you to trust Him over your fears? How can God's "Fear not" reminders make a difference in your decisions today?

BE THE MAN
WHO WELCOMES
FORGIVENESS

But Zacchaeus stood up and said to the Lord, "Look, Lord! Here and now I give half of my possessions to the poor, and if I have cheated anybody out of anything, I will pay back four times the amount."

LUKE 19:8 NIV

Luke 19 shares the story of a man who was short on strength. He'd taken on a job that found him collecting tax from his friends and neighbors. In his weakness, he decided to start overcalculating their tax. . .and pocketing the difference. This bad idea, of course, didn't go unnoticed. Soon, Zacchaeus also became short on friends.

One day, Jesus came to town. But when the local buzz pinpointed the street where He'd walk, nobody bothered to save Zacchaeus a space. As a result, the tax collector decided to climb a tree. There, he'd have one of the best views in town!

When Jesus was about to pass by, He stopped under the tree, looked up, and invited Himself to dinner. It was at that meal that Jesus confronted Zacchaeus' weak actions. Somehow, instead of fearfully retreating, this man gained strength from Jesus' words. He changed his thinking and then his actions. He stopped collecting extra tax and provided a refund to everyone he'd taken advantage of.

This unique story is a powerful example of what happens when a man comes to grips with a hard truth, abandons fear, and seeks God's strength. Don't fear being called out by God. Instead, accept His assessment of your weakness and embrace the strength He offers. Don't get mad because you were caught in sin—rejoice because Forgiveness came to town and noticed you.

Why does correction often lead to defensiveness? How can God's assessment of your actions lead to greater inner strength?

BE THE MAN
WHO ACCEPTS HIS TEAM

I am the good shepherd: the good shepherd giveth his life for the sheep.

JOHN 10:11 KJV

Sports teams usually choose mascots that evoke feelings of strength. That's why they pick animals like bears, lions, and eagles over creatures like sloths, groundhogs, and naked mole rats. We all want a strong representation of what we believe in.

If you believe in fear, what's the mascot for that? This may seem like an absurd question, but you'd be surprised by how many men choose to live in fear rather than the strength that comes with faith in God.

One of the most fear-prone animals in the world is a sheep. Most people find it hard to get behind that kind of mascot, yet the Bible repeatedly compares us to these frightened creatures. But you know what other qualities sheep have? They stay calm in the presence of their shepherd. Similarly, we're all hopelessly fearful, but we have direct access to the God who has enough strength for all.

There are three types of people: those who are strong because God made them strong, those who are weak because they haven't accepted His strength, and those who are getting weaker because they've been spending too much time away from the sheep pen. (Talk about a fearful experience!)

As a Christian, you exist on Team Sheep. . .but your mascot is a Lion—which represents God Himself.

God is also the coach. No one is stronger than Him. No one can best Him. He treats His team with great respect. And when you're weak, just remember who is strong. God can help you.

How do you feel about the idea of being on Team Sheep? What is the right time to seek God's help when you're afraid? Why?

BE THE MAN
WHO TRADES WEAKNESS FOR STRENGTH

Now all glory to God, who is able, through his mighty power at work within us, to accomplish infinitely more than we might ask or think.

EPHESIANS 3:20 NLT

We remember people who go above and beyond. Those who don't have to help but do it anyway. Those who lend their expertise without being asked. Those who jump to carry others' burdens, choosing to walk with them shoulder to shoulder.

But sometimes, going above and beyond is impossible, no matter how hard you try. You can barely take care of yourself, let alone help someone through a tough time. In these times, who's remembering you? God. (No surprise there.)

He knows the struggle you face. But He also knows that when you want to check out, the real answer is to check in with Him. He goes above and beyond for you. He helps, lends expertise, and stands with you.

The strength you need isn't found in a gym, an energy drink, or a list of all-natural vitamins. No, you benefit from a very unfair trade. It can feel like trading in an old, broken-down station wagon for a brand-new luxury SUV. The deal is straight across with no payments and free maintenance for life.

God wants your anxiety and worry—in exchange, He offers strength and peace. Sound too good to be true? Rest assured: it's true. God calls this gift *grace*. It's more than you deserve, but it's just one set of gifts God gives to help you live a thriving life, even in the soil of personal disappointment.

Be a strong man who started out weak. Accept the strength trade today.

Have you accepted God's gift of strength and given up your willingness to stay weak? How does this trade seem better than what you deserve?

BE THE MAN
WHO RESPONDS
APPROPRIATELY

Cast all your anxiety on him because he cares for you.

1 PETER 5:7 NIV

Imagine for a minute that it's the Fourth of July. Rockets, roman candles, and fountains glow in unison as America celebrates its independence. The skies light up and fireworks boom, harkening back to a time of wars fought and won. Some, trying their hand at photography, capture the display with cell phones. *Oohs* and *aahs* flow from the lips of the thrilled.

Within each house, pets cower under beds, certain the world is coming to an end. Most will get over the trauma. . .others will not. Every time a fork is dropped in the kitchen, they'll race to a hiding spot and visibly shake, remembering that horrid night of danger. Some behavior will look a bit like PTSD.

Now, this isn't a public service announcement for pets. Instead, it's meant to paint a picture of what anxiety can do to you when you have no idea what's happening. The noise of life can instill a fight or flight response that's hardly ever appropriate.

Difficult days are a part of life, so you'll inevitably face some things you can't understand. It may seem as if your world is ending or that your life is spiraling toward devastation. God knows you're worried. He gets it. That's why He says once more that you should hand this bit of dirty laundry to Him. He'll give you better things to wear.

Be a man who possesses the kind of strength that only God can offer.

Why is it important to remember that God's care for you is bigger than your fears? Does your fear and anxiety seem a bit like dirty laundry?

BE THE MAN
WHO ACCEPTS
GOD'S CONDITIONS

Barak said unto her, If thou wilt go with me, then I will go:
but if thou wilt not go with me, then I will not go.

JUDGES 4:8 KJV

Every good story has a villain. As for the story in Judges 4, this villain was a cruel man named Sisera. To battle this brash adversary, God had raised up a warrior named Barak.

In other words: Sisera, bad; Barak, good.

So if God chose Barak and Barak was good, then Sisera didn't stand a chance against God's chosen warrior, right? But Barak had a choice to make. . .and his choice didn't fit his calling.

Deborah was a prophetess, and she came to Barak to tell him that God was sending him to win the battle against Sisera. And if God does the sending, you'd better believe the battle is in God's "win" column. However, Barak's response was essentially "Um, I'm not going unless you come with me."

So just to be clear—God chose Barak, told him He

would be with him, and asked him to go win a battle. All Barak needed to do was show up and claim a victory. But he couldn't do it. Consequently, Barak had to settle for being a mere footnote in Deborah's story.

God wants you to shed anxiety so that you can wear His strength. He promises to go with you. This isn't a game of wait and see—His presence will *always* be enough.

Be a man who accepts God's strength. When you need it, He'll supply it. All you've got to do is step up.

Do you ever try to place conditions on God's offer of strength? Has God ever failed to keep His promises?

BE THE MAN
WHO'S AMAZED BY GOD'S STRENGTH

The LORD made the earth by his power, and he preserves it by his wisdom. With his own understanding he stretched out the heavens. When he speaks in the thunder, the heavens roar with rain. He causes the clouds to rise over the earth. He sends the lightning with the rain and releases the wind from his storehouses.

JEREMIAH 10:12–13 NLT

Talk to a meteorologist long enough, and you'll hear things like "a strong mid-level warm air advection will be aided by an upper-level divergence" and "a vigorous upper-level trough may erode the mid-level warm pool." These seemingly incomprehensible phrases, however, usually boil down to something like "It's going to be a nice day" or "Watch out for storms this evening."

You don't have to understand the language of a meteorologist to know that weather can be crazy. Whether it's lightning, thunder, rain, hail, wind, or snow, you can't control the weather. No matter how many times you revert to childhood and sing, "Rain, rain, go away. Come again some other day," the weather doesn't care. All that'll do is confuse and annoy the people at the local convenience store who are waiting out the storm.

Weather is a powerful reminder of God's strength. He created weather and now preserves it, even when it gets severe. He tells thunder when it's time to boom. He tells lightning when it's time for a real display. He even has a storehouse for wind.

When you are going through your own seasons of trouble, try focusing on a storm in your past that's been long overshadowed by sunny days. Then remember this one truth: God is bigger than any storm, no matter how ferocious.

Does weather cause you to trust God more? How can it remind you of God's strength?

BE THE MAN
WHO CELEBRATES
GOD'S STRENGTH

Then God said, "Let us make mankind in our image, in our likeness."

GENESIS 1:26 NIV

Director Frank Capra delivered a movie in the mid-1940s that did little to capture the attention of moviegoers at the time. The movie might've been forgotten entirely if it hadn't been picked up by television and replayed every Christmas.

The story follows Jimmy Stewart's character, George, as he experiences many troubles and setbacks. All his dreams seem to end in disappointment. One day, he decides he's had enough—but just before George can make a terrible decision, a self-described angel arrives to show him what life would be like without him.

As it turns out, George's trouble has brought strength not only to himself but to those around him. Without him, things are much worse. The town's name is changed, and everyone is somehow harder and more calloused.

Unfortunately, this beloved movie has no real-life counterpart. You can't really look at what life would be like without you. And even if you tried to speculate, your faulty conclusions might make you even more depressed!

However, maybe your pity party can transform into a celebration if you pay attention to the things God has said about you. He made you, He loves you, and He sent His Son to die for you. He created you with a purpose, making you a part of His grand plan. He has chosen to be with you, and He'll never leave. He wants to impact the world with your life—a story only you can share.

God wants to make the world a better place because you are here. He has a plan for you—will you cooperate?

How is strength linked to God's purpose for you? Why should pity parties always give way to celebrations of God's goodness?

BE THE MAN
WHO ISN'T A LONE WOLF

Two are better than one; because they have a good reward for their labour.

ECCLESIASTES 4:9 KJV

Does the idea of being a lone wolf appeal to you? Going it alone sounds like something men are supposed to do. Pulling yourself up by your bootstraps seems like a worthy story to share with grandchildren. Self-reliance seems like something to be proud of.

Yet God has created you for relationship. Friendships are important. Shared burdens result in efficiency. Working with someone brings encouragement. Receiving help boosts your confidence for the task at hand.

A great illustration can be found in a very unusual object: the disposable diaper. Because these diapers contain a certain polymer, they have uses that most people never consider. Perhaps the strangest: you can use a new diaper as your antiperspirant! Because the diaper is absorbent and has a fresh scent, it's helpful for drying things out and leaving you smelling fresh all day long. Other uses include keeping cut flowers fresh, preventing fires, and improving the hardness of cement.

Peanut butter complements chocolate, marshmallows complement hot cocoa, and tacos complement almost anything. Who's complementing you? Do you have a friend who just seems to make you better?

These questions are not meant to minimize God's strength but to point out one of the ways He can strengthen you. Knowing that someone has your back can change the way you feel about any challenge. Confidence comes when friends stand together.

Why do you think God made friendships so important? Do you have an "Ecclesiastes 4:9" friend? Can you be one?

BE THE MAN
WHO KNOWS
WHEN TO HUSH

Then they sat on the ground with him for seven days and nights. No one said a word to Job, for they saw that his suffering was too great for words.

JOB 2:13 NLT

Sometimes, the worst thing you can do for someone is talk. You see someone struggling and you want to help, so you fill the silence with words that only end up causing pain.

Guys are wired to be fixers. If you can come up with a solution for what's bothering a friend, then you can put it behind you and move on as if nothing were ever wrong. But often, this "solution" is just a best guess. . .and that's not what friends need. Sometimes, they just need to hear these four words: "I'm here for you."

Job's friends started that way. They recognized his suffering was too big for words to heal. But the longer they endured silence, the more awkward they likely felt. You know what that's like. You meet a friend who's quiet, and it isn't long before the silence gets to be too much. Your jaw suddenly unhinges, spilling out obviously unhelpful words, but you can't make it stop. The words flow as freely as opinions at Thanksgiving dinner, and the awkwardness explodes.

Just like adult children who don't want their parent's advice unless they ask for it, so too are your hurting friends. They might need a friend who's content to just be there for them. You can add or diminish strength based on what you choose—or refuse—to say.

Why is it so hard to wait in silence? How can ongoing conversations diminish strength?

BE THE MAN
WHO RECOGNIZES
STRENGTH'S VALUE

"The LORD will guide you always; he will satisfy your needs in a sun-scorched land and will strengthen your frame. You will be like a well-watered garden, like a spring whose waters never fail."

ISAIAH 58:11 NIV

Excessive worry prevents you from enjoying life. "But," you may say, "being pessimistic means I'm never disappointed." Fair enough. But even if you're wrong and good things do come, you immediately assume this good fortune won't last.

Instead of enhancing life, worry makes it much smaller. It taps into today's strength and bleeds it dry. And when you throw what little strength you have left to the wind, worry will come back again tomorrow.

But who wants a small life? Who wants their life to shrink like cooked bacon? Who looks at their deficiencies and thinks, *I want even less*? If you're one of the millions who would shout, "No one!" then there is good news. You don't have to settle for a life with fewer opportunities and minimal satisfaction.

You don't have to settle for "runt-of-the-litter" living. If God supplies abundantly, stop behaving like you're living in spiritual poverty. If He loves, stop acting like you're rejected. If He lives, stop assuming there's no hope.

It's easy to tell the difference between a well-nurtured garden and an abandoned one. If your life is a garden, don't set up an umbrella when God sends the rain.

Strength is easy to lose, but it can also be replenished. You can make strength-depleting choices, but don't forget the choices that bring restoration. God can provide more than you started with.

What might cause you to release your grip on strength? Why can that sometimes seem like a good option? Why is that a lie?

BE THE MAN
WHO AVOIDS
WRONG PLACES

Blessed is the man that walketh not in the counsel of the ungodly, nor standeth in the way of sinners, nor sitteth in the seat of the scornful. But his delight is in the law of the Lord; and in his law doth he meditate day and night. And he shall be like a tree planted by the rivers of water, that bringeth forth his fruit in his season; his leaf also shall not wither; and whatsoever he doeth shall prosper.

PSALM 1:1–3 KJV

Weakness comes when you walk, stand, or sit in the wrong place. It's not really a matter of location—it's a matter of company. It can be exhausting to spend your time with "spiritual leeches" who seem bent on ridding you of spiritual strength.

God says you're a blessed man if you let Him steer you away from these ungodly scorners and toward His Word instead. It's like being a tree that's transplanted from the arid desert to the edge of a rushing river. The first fights for every available ounce of strength; the second grows mighty through abundance.

Choosing generosity in place of selfishness has the same effect. Have you ever seen the satisfaction on someone's face when that person gives a gift that's well received? When someone goes out of their way to help someone who needs it? This type of action transforms people from weak and malnourished to strong and thriving.

A man's strength depends on where he walks, stands, and sits. Weakness always follows the wrong choice. But there's good news—God can fix that too.

Have you ever witnessed the weakness that comes from having the wrong companions? How can God's Word lead you toward improved strength?

BE THE MAN
WHO OPENS HIS TOOLBOX

Tell them to use their money to do good. They should be rich in good works and generous to those in need, always being ready to share with others. By doing this they will be storing up their treasure as a good foundation for the future so that they may experience true life.

1 TIMOTHY 6:18–19 NLT

Spiritual math is strange. Somehow, you can take God's strength, give His strength to those who need it, and walk away with more than you started with!

God doesn't forbid spending time with nonbelievers. He actually wants you to help them. But there's a big difference between using His strength to introduce people to Him and merely joining the crowd described in Psalm 1—the ungodly, sinners, and scornful. Even among non-Christians, you stick with God's agenda. You don't relax your standards or let down your guard. Your strength diminishes when you decide to use God's Great Commission as an invitation to jump back into the life you wisely left. If you aren't with the unbelieving to extend the offer of God's rescue, then it may be time to get out. The longer you stay, the weaker you'll become.

But when you take the right approach, everything from your finances to your presence can be a tool that God uses. Your generosity and readiness to help will get people asking why. When you do this, 1 Timothy 6 says that you are storing up treasure, building a good foundation and experiencing true life.

Men of strength understand they're on a mission. They know their choices have consequences, their actions have reactions, and their strength can always improve.

Why does God care if you store, build, and experience the right things? How can you prioritize God's commission and then seek the strength to do what He asks?

BE THE MAN
WHO FINDS SECURITY

You created my inmost being; you knit me together in my mother's womb. . . . Your eyes saw my unformed body; all the days ordained for me were written in your book before one of them came to be.

PSALM 139:13, 16 NIV

Every man who's ever existed has one thing in common—*insecurity*. Some are better at masking it than others, but all men ask themselves at some point, "Do I measure up?" You want to know if you fit into a plan—any plan. You want to know if your life is going to impact someone—anyone. You want to know if God ever thinks about you—any thoughts.

Psalm 139 is your answer. Before your body even had form, God stitched you together. He knew how long you'd live before you took a breath. He's got a book with your story written inside. None of your choices take Him by surprise. He knows the path you should take before you think to ask.

If you are insecure, take heart: your perspective can

change. You don't have to wonder if you are important to God. You can be secure knowing that you are. . .and always have been.

Your insecurity is not unique, even if you deny it exists. God's got a lock on security, and He says you obtain that security when you obtain Him. If you don't have Him, you don't have security.

You were not an accident—you were created. You were not unknown—God saw you. You are not unrecognized—God has a book with your story.

A man of strength first understands his weakness, and then he understands that insecurity is nothing more than a terminated position—a career God has replaced with trust.

How does insecurity play a role in your view of life? Do you find it easy to deny your insecurity? Why is it important to admit that you are sometimes insecure?

BE THE MAN
WHO DOESN'T BETRAY
THE BETRAYER

It is not an enemy who taunts me—I could bear that. It is not my foes who so arrogantly insult me—I could have hidden from them. Instead, it is you—my equal, my companion and close friend. What good fellowship we once enjoyed as we walked together to the house of God.

Psalm 55:12-14 NLT

Betrayal can't come from an enemy—you have to be friends first. Betrayal does the unthinkable because it's an act you don't expect.

Nestled a third of the way through the book of Psalms is a chapter (Psalm 55) that deals with a betrayal David once had. David lamented that it was more bearable to have an enemy taunt him (remember Goliath?) than a friend. A foe could insult him, but it was more damaging from someone he thought he could trust.

When the one who knows your secrets shares them, trust dissolves. When that person lies about you, a friendship is broken. When a friend insults you, a storehouse of good memories is shaken out into a violent wind. It's hard to recover from a betrayal. It hurts. It leaves you weak. It makes you ponder all the things you would've done differently if you'd known then what you know now. You can no longer recommend that person for a job in good conscience, and you might secretly hope God will return the favor to this former friend. Even worse, you might try to take matters into your own hands, and the accumulated anger will leave you spiritually bankrupt.

When God says to pray for your enemies—to refuse to repay evil for evil—it's not because He wants to let them off the hook. Rather, He doesn't want you to place yourself on a brand-new hook. Their betrayal doesn't modify God's orders.

Why is it easy to seek an evil end for a betrayer? How can you process the pain of betrayal to discover a better answer?

BE THE MAN
WHO LETS GOD JUDGE

When they hurled their insults at him, he did not retaliate; when he suffered, he made no threats. Instead, he entrusted himself to him who judges justly.

1 PETER 2:23 NIV

It's the theme of countless movies and TV shows: revenge. To borrow a phrase from 1970s singer B. J. Thomas, "somebody done somebody wrong"—and the second somebody's going to make the first one pay.

As Christian men, we know that Jesus taught His followers to "love your enemies and pray for those who persecute you" (Matthew 5:44 NIV). Why? "That you may be children of your Father in heaven" (verse 45 NIV).

But even as Christian men, we're very much a part of this broken world. We don't even need the influence of thousands of hours of movies and TV shows to make us want revenge. . .though all those "I'll get you back" story lines certainly haven't helped.

A true man of strength, however, does not pursue vengeance. He knows that the Lord has said, "It is mine to avenge; I will repay" (Romans 12:19 NIV). He knows that even Jesus, the perfect, all-knowing, all-powerful God, chose not to lash out at the people who were killing Him. He never threatened or retaliated, though He could have wiped out His enemies with a sniff, a blink, or the flick of the hand. Instead, Jesus "entrusted himself to him who judges justly"—God the Father.

Vengeance makes for an exciting climax to a movie. But in real life, it generates even more pain and trouble. The strong man is the one who—like his Lord—leaves the paybacks in God's hands.

How does knowing Jesus was betrayed help you rethink your reactions to a betrayer? Why is God's judgment worth more than any other opinion?

BE THE MAN
WHO NEVER GIVES UP

Think of all the hostility he endured from sinful people; then you won't become weary and give up.

There is a spiritual song from the 1880s that still strikes a chord with those who hear it. It goes like this:

> *Nobody knows the trouble I've seen,*
> *Nobody knows but Jesus.*
> *Nobody knows the trouble I've seen,*
> *Glory, Hallelujah.*
> *Sometimes I'm up,*
> *Sometimes I'm down,*
> *Oh, yes, Lord,*
> *Sometimes I'm almost to the ground,*
> *Oh, yes, Lord.*

To better understand why Jesus would know our troubles, please read Hebrews 12:3 again. Strength must come through endurance, and Jesus showed the world how to do that. He endured hostilities, lies, insults, threats, beatings, and even death. He went further than anyone had ever gone for you. He endured more pain and humiliation than you ever will. That's why you can gain strength from these eight words: "Then you won't become weary and give up."

Weakness is a close companion to weariness, and throwing in the towel is an admission of defeat. It says, "I can't go on like this. All my enemies can now declare victory because this fight is over!"

Your struggles may be unique to you—sometimes, you may feel driven almost "to the ground." But Jesus knows. . .and He cares.

Oh, yes, Lord. Glory, hallelujah!

When you are weary, do you sometimes think your problem is unique? How can you gain strength by remembering Jesus endured all of your suffering—and then some?

BE THE MAN
WHO GAINS STRENGTH
IN THE TELLING

"Give his people the knowledge of salvation through the forgiveness of their sins."

LUKE 1:77 NIV

Before Jesus gave the Great Commission, John the Baptist told people to turn away from sin and toward a friendship with God. And before John the Baptist was born, his father, Zechariah, who was a priest, spoke the words written in Luke 1:77.

God was Jesus' father, but Zechariah would've been known as Jesus' uncle. The Bible doesn't say how close John and Jesus were, but they shared the same message—God's salvation must come through forgiveness. This forgiveness inspires strength because it releases guilt, restores hope, and mends your broken relationship with God.

If forgiveness does all that, why would you keep it to yourself? You might feel comfortable and safe in the silence. You might assume telling others about Jesus is a job for someone else. But after Jesus rose from the dead, every disciple kept telling this amazing truth. If those who heard and believed had stopped adding links to the information chain, it would have been broken centuries ago. But that didn't happen. The strength of the message continues to be shared by people like you.

This strength comes in two forms: (1) the strength God gives you to share His amazing gift and (2) the strength you receive from speaking about it.

A man of strength accepts God's boldness and then embraces the strength that comes when he shares "the knowledge of salvation through the forgiveness of. . .sins."

Today, gain strength in the telling.

Have you ever experienced this two-tier gift of strength by telling people about Jesus? If so, what did you learn?

BE THE MAN
WHO BUILDS
WITH SUCCESS

They go from strength to strength.

PSALM 84:7 KJV

God's strength may seem like an impossible acquisition.

Matthew 25 contains the story of three men who were managers of their employer's business holdings. The boss gave all three a certain amount of money to invest while he was away. Two of these men managed to double their investment. (The Bible doesn't say how.) One success led to more success as they wisely used what they were given. The third, however, essentially put the cash in his mattress. He chose to live in fear of his employer, making inaction his permanent address.

Psalm 84 echoes this story's theme when it describes success as a grand procession. This chapter is all about a journey to God, so it's fitting that the idea of one strength leading to another strength is found in the middle of the Psalms near the center of the Bible.

This procession is all about victory and

overcoming—about honoring a good God who offers free samples of strength for those who start their spiritual journey and keeps growing it from there. So bring on the celebration!

Building blocks of God's strength are assembled through acts of trust. Without trust, we're left with nothing but weakness. Our "God blocks" fall apart, replaced by the fear we thought we'd left behind so long ago.

So today, be a man who accepts God's strength. Don't even think of going without it.

Does it help you to think of accepting God's strength one challenge at a time? How might one moment of God's strength lead to a stronger life of faith?

BE THE MAN
WHO ABANDONS
HIS OLD ADDRESS

My old self has been crucified with Christ. It is no longer I who live, but Christ lives in me. So I live in this earthly body by trusting in the Son of God, who loved me and gave himself for me.

GALATIANS 2:20 NLT

When you sell your house or move out of a rental property, it's natural to take all your belongings. You don't leave some things just in case you want to go back someday, and you don't leave one room untouched so that you'll have a place to visit. No, you take everything. Why? Because your address has changed. The old house is no longer home. You don't live there anymore.

This is how we should treat the separation between our old life and the new. Yet too often, we find ourselves knocking on the door to a house that's no longer ours, wanting to spend time with things we left behind. We won't find strength in this dilapidated place—only fear at every turn. The doors creak and so do the floors. This shack doesn't even feel like home, so why do we spend so much time here?

Strength is found when we move forward in our friendship with God. When we leave the past in the past and know our future lies elsewhere. When we resist the urge to turn from God's provision back to the weakness that no longer defines us.

You may know you have a different future, but emotions can make you think there's something special you've left behind. Any return you make, however, will be a less-than-satisfying reunion. So do everything you can to remember why you left it in the past—your feet weren't made to walk that path again.

When do you feel the pull to revisit your past life the most? Why is it important to resist a return?

BE THE MAN
WHO ESCAPES
HIS IMAGINATION

"Do not worry about your life, what you will eat or drink; or about your body, what you will wear. Is not life more than food, and the body more than clothes?"

MATTHEW 6:25 NIV

Walter Mitty is the fictional protagonist of two movies bearing his name. In both stories, he has a mediocre job and is rather clumsy and confused. All his strength comes through his fantastical daydreams. But when Walter finally engages with reality, the shackles of his imagination grow less powerful. The worry he once embraced is transformed into strength.

When you stop looking at all the "what ifs" in life and pay attention to "what *is*," there'll be a big shift in how you perceive things. This is no substitute for God's strength; instead, it's a great way to stop working against God and continually insisting that life is against you.

Worry is worthless—God's Word says so. If you're thirsty, there's water. If you need clothes, there are plenty of shops to choose from. Life is more than a designer label or a packaged bottle of water. When you get mired in the specifics, you miss out on the adventure happening all around you. You start looking like a detective who's carrying the world's largest magnifying glass.

As a man of strength, you can cooperate with God. So take your thoughts captive and interrogate them in the light of God's Word—not the faulty glow of your imagination.

How often have you allowed your imagination to convince you things are worse than they actually are? When was the last time you measured your thoughts using the Bible's teachings? How might you use this strategy more?

BE THE MAN
WHO CONTROLS
HIS WORRY

*"Don't worry about tomorrow, for tomorrow will bring its
own worries. Today's trouble is enough for today."*

MATTHEW 6:34 NLT

Anxiety is universal. All people face it, and all people have
their own ideas about how to deal with it. One high-
profile personality combats anxiety by working harder.
Another writes every bit of anxiety down on a piece of
paper and then burns it. And one animal farm in Colorado
has teamed up with local schools to help children reduce
their anxiety through an animal pen pal program.

But God has a simpler method: don't worry.

"Easier said than done," you might say. You have a long
list of things to worry about: the climate, your finances,
your children, your parents, a job, a vehicle, a virus, a
strange dog—you name it. And no one would fault you
for that. Everyone knows worry is a strength eliminator.

But God still says, "Don't worry."

You can spend so much time on red alert crisis mode

about bad things that *might* happen that you miss the good things that actually *do*. Ironically, this causes you to miss everything that could've given you strength, thus leading to extreme fatigue and a propensity to get even more frustrated next time.

Today, make worry take a back seat to your plans. A man of strength realizes he can't control everything. He knows bad things can and do happen, but he also knows he doesn't need to witness every bad thing when good things are happening each day. Strength returns when you seek God's good news.

Do you find it easy to let worry consume the good parts of your day? How might you challenge worry to take a back seat?

BE THE MAN
WHO RECOGNIZES
THE RIGHT HAND

Fear thou not; for I am with thee: be not dismayed; for I am thy God: I will strengthen thee; yea, I will help thee; yea, I will uphold thee with the right hand of my righteousness.

Isaiah 41:10 KJV

No matter which part of your body you want to strengthen—hair, immune system, or muscles—there's a plethora of vitamins or dietary programs for you to choose from. But if you want to strengthen your spirit and soul, God is your only option.

What's the value of a healthy body if you have a weak spirit? It just means you'll look better than you feel. It means settling for the lesser of two strengths. . .which just amounts to weakness.

You could strike out on your own, or you could stay in God's care. The first might lead to disaster; the second is a solid foundation. The first is stubbornly refusing to follow directions and getting lost; the second is following God's GPS—the Holy Spirit—who will lead you down the right path.

Once you realize that God has poured every resource imaginable into guiding you home, there's no room for distress. Be strengthened by that bit of good news.

But what if you've gotten so used to being weak that it seems uncomfortable to see yourself as strong? You see, a man infused with God's strength isn't concerned with impressing others—he's just impressed with the God who actually gave him strength. When your strength comes from God, it's a controlled and compassionate strength that helps you and everyone else.

Do you sometimes choose weakness over strength?
Why is it wise to accept God's strength?

BE THE MAN
WHO REDEFINES *NEED*

God will generously provide all you need. Then you will always have everything you need and plenty left over to share with others.

2 CORINTHIANS 9:8 NLT

What if you never had to worry about whether your life could be successful? What if strength was assured? What if you knew all your needs would be supplied? How would the answers to these three questions change the way you live?

Good news: with God, those questions are already answered! But it's human nature to still phrase them as a "what if." And this uncertainty keeps messing with our ability to feel secure. We want assurances (and God gives them), but we can't seem to believe this kind of security exists. We've experienced the feeling of seemingly not having what we need, and we hate this feeling so much that it's hard for us to leave our life in someone else's hands.

So when we read 2 Corinthians 9:8, we might

ask—with just a touch of sarcasm—"So what's the catch?" Phrases like "everything you need" and "plenty left over" make us wonder if God's taken a look at our bank account lately.

But *need* doesn't have a fixed definition in the human mind. Today, you might believe you need a car. But there was a time when cars didn't exist, so no one ever felt they needed them. Universal needs include things like air, water, food, love, hope, and forgiveness. But were those the things you thought of when you read the word *need*?

God knew you would need Him, and He meets that need every day. If you adjust your list of true needs, you'll see God has never failed to meet them.

Do you let God decide what you really need? How might readjusting the way you think of need change the way you think of God?

BE THE MAN
WHO WISELY ENLISTS

Fight the good fight of the faith. Take hold of the eternal life to which you were called when you made your good confession in the presence of many witnesses.

1 TIMOTHY 6:12 NIV

Is surrender a sign of weakness or strength. . .or both?

Think of a soldier. For this soldier, surrendering to the enemy would be a sign of weakness. But each day, the same soldier must surrender his own plans and desires to the orders of his commander. That's a sign of strength.

So for a soldier, the second kind of surrender happens first. After that, *surrender* becomes a foreign word. In the same way, you were called to fight a good and faithful fight for God. And when you love God, there's no need to back down. When you serve God, there's no need to call in sick. When God tells you to stand, you stand. You follow a new plan, so the thought of abandoning your post should never cross your mind.

People pay attention to your new life—they want to see how it works for you. If you walk away, it might cause the observer to conclude that God can't really change anything. In that instance, God gets blamed for your choice. How fair is that?

A man of strength—a true Christian soldier—understands that what he abandoned will never be worth more than the companionship of other soldiers. He also knows that being a soldier isn't about physical strength—it's about agreeing to follow and obey the God he enlisted to serve.

His reward? An existence that never ends, even after he breathes his last.

Why must you surrender to God before you can refuse to surrender to anything else? Why is the battle cry of "No surrender" an appropriate response for God's soldiers?

BE THE MAN
WHO SEPARATES
KNOWLEDGE FROM WISDOM

"God also gave Joseph unusual wisdom, so that Pharaoh appointed him governor over all of Egypt and put him in charge of the palace."

ACTS 7:10 NLT

Wisdom is an important aspect of strength. Acting foolish, on the other hand, is usually seen as weakness. You can know lots of stuff and still be considered foolish. Why? Because wisdom is knowing what to do with what you know. Knowledge is not just useful for winning trivia games—it's essential for making quality decisions.

One of those wise men found in the Bible is Joseph. This man was the second youngest of his brothers, who all hated him and sold him into slavery. After being sold into slavery, he was accused of a crime he didn't commit, placed in jail, and forgotten by the only man who could've helped secure his release. Not exactly the best soil for wisdom to grow! But the Bible says God was with Joseph through it all.

In fact, God's strength, found in the "unusual wisdom" of Joseph, was instrumental in turning his bad circumstances into incredible outcomes. By the time the story reaches its pinnacle, the worst famine in recent memory was raging. . .and Joseph was the second in command of an entire country. The wisdom God gave him allowed him to implement a national rationing plan that saved people from many countries. And when Joseph had the chance to pay his brothers back, his God-given wisdom led him to do something unexpected instead— he gave them a new home in Egypt, where they'd have enough food to withstand the bad years.

How might you explain the difference between wisdom and knowledge? Why should you gain strength from God's wisdom?

BE THE MAN
WHO SEES BEYOND
"AVERAGE"

Then the LORD said to Moses, "See, I have chosen Bezalel son of Uri, the son of Hur, of the tribe of Judah, and I have filled him with the Spirit of God, with wisdom, with understanding, with knowledge and with all kinds of skills—to make artistic designs for work in gold, silver and bronze, to cut and set stones, to work in wood, and to engage in all kinds of crafts."

EXODUS 31:1–5 NIV

People can, intentionally or unintentionally, place workers in categories. If a man works in an office, people may see him as more important than one who wears a hard hat and gets his hands dirty. They might even assume there's an intelligence gap between the two. This distinction usually isn't said aloud, and some might not even be aware they're making it.

Exodus 31 doesn't say a lot about Bezalel, but we do know he was someone who worked with his hands. He probably had callused hands and dirt beneath his broken fingernails. Yet God did something remarkable. He didn't dismiss this hardworking man or indicate he had no value. No, He specifically told Moses that this man was important. God said, "I have filled him with the Spirit of God, with wisdom, with understanding, with knowledge and with all kinds of skills."

This man's skill was inspired by the God who created everything. God Himself gave this artisan the ability to create with wisdom.

Today, gain strength and perspective from this lesser-known Bible man, knowing that God has a plan for you as well.

Why is it easy to place people in different categories based on their occupation? Why is this perspective shortsighted?

BE THE MAN
WHO RECOGNIZES
GOD'S STRENGTH

There is a man in thy kingdom, in whom is the spirit of the holy gods; and in the days of thy father light and understanding and wisdom, like the wisdom of the gods, was found in him; . . .forasmuch as an excellent spirit, and knowledge, and understanding, interpreting of dreams, and shewing of hard sentences, and dissolving of doubts, were found in the same Daniel, whom the king named Belteshazzar: now let Daniel be called.

DANIEL 5:11-12 KJV

Daniel was a man who, at any point, could probably be voted as the smartest in the room. Of course, God was wiser than Daniel, but Daniel was sold out to following God—so God gave him a wisdom that was unmatched in the world at the time.

When Daniel spoke, he calmed fear and inspired trust with his convincing arguments. He understood the world around him and the God who made that world. God even helped him interpret dreams. Daniel's lifelong pursuit of God put him in the ranks of the wisest men who've ever lived. As those around him immersed themselves in a smelly marinade of jealousy, spite, and vindictiveness—trying their best to ruin the reputation of a good man—Daniel stood out as a man of strength. Feel free to read the book of Daniel to see who succeeded.

A man of strength knows that his "God wisdom" doesn't depend on the opinions of the jealous, spiteful, and vindictive. These people don't like anything that reminds them of their imperfection. God's wisdom can do that. It's also the thing that points them toward a strength that only God can supply.

How can becoming wise make you more aware of God's strength? Do you employ this wisdom in your everyday life?

BE THE MAN
WHO SPEAKS ONLY TRUTH

Stephen, a man full of God's grace and power, performed amazing miracles and signs among the people. But one day some men from the Synagogue of Freed Slaves, as it was called, started to debate with him. They were Jews from Cyrene, Alexandria, Cilicia, and the province of Asia. None of them could stand against the wisdom and the Spirit with which Stephen spoke.

ACTS 6:8-10 NLT

How do you react when you are confronted with a truth that opposes your actions and plans? When pitted against conventional wisdom, truth wins. . .but this victory is hardly ever easy to accept.

Imagine a group of men who arrived from various parts of the world. They thought they were pretty smart, so when they heard about Stephen, they organized a public debate. These well-traveled men would show the world how smart they were and why it was foolish to listen to Stephen's words. Each of their arguments was perfectly designed to crush Stephen and debunk what he had to say about Jesus. It would be a courtroom smackdown for the ages.

Stephen, however, had some impressive credentials too. He possessed grace and power. He performed miracles. So when this tag team of at least four men showed up to put Stephen in his place, they were rudely surprised. Because they didn't possess God's wisdom, they in turn missed out on God's strength: "None of them could stand against the wisdom and the Spirit with which Stephen spoke."

God's strength was manifested through Stephen's firm conviction. It showed up because he refused to accept any pet theory that contradicted God's wisdom by even the smallest degree.

How can accepting God's truth to the exclusion of all other wisdom improve your spiritual strength? Have you accepted this truth?

BE THE MAN
WHO DISMISSES
FOOLISHNESS

God has made the wisdom of this world look foolish. Since God in his wisdom saw to it that the world would never know him through human wisdom, he has used our foolish preaching to save those who believe. It is foolish to the Jews, who ask for signs from heaven. And it is foolish to the Greeks, who seek human wisdom. So when we preach that Christ was crucified, the Jews are offended and the Gentiles say it's all nonsense.

1 CORINTHIANS 1:20–23 NLT

You might've heard parents or grandparents tell you that if you swallow bubble gum, it won't digest for years. That cracking your knuckles when you're young will give you arthritis. That carrots make your eyesight better. That you shouldn't shave your hair because it makes it come back thicker.

It turns out, these bits of wisdom (and dozens like them) aren't true. You might have believed them because they were told to you by people you trust. You had no reason not to trust those people—they just had an incomplete picture of the truth about gum, knuckles, carrots, and hair.

When someone comes to you with statistics, scientific research, or even a parent's supposed wisdom, you expect facts from that person. But in the end, this wisdom might well prove to be no more than foolishness.

Many of those same people might dismiss statements like "God exists," "God loves people," and "Jesus offers forgiveness." They see these ideas as foolish and misguided, even though what they're hearing is *true* wisdom indeed!

A man of strength understands that guesses can't override what God says is true.

Why does disbelief in God make no sense? Which do you prioritize: God's truth or the daily news?

BE THE MAN
WHO USES HIS
GIFT WISELY

There are different kinds of gifts, but the same Spirit distributes them. There are different kinds of service, but the same Lord. There are different kinds of working, but in all of them and in everyone it is the same God at work.

1 CORINTHIANS 12:4–6 NIV

Did you read the passage above? Good, now reread it. These verses describe action. There's nothing passive or wishy-washy here. This is no folklore to research and disprove. Today's big truth is that God has given you a unique gift based on your passions and identity. Your purpose in life is linked to that gift, so pursuing the best use of this gift is another way that God will give you strength.

Lots of gifts are available, and different people have access to different gifts. But each gift comes from God—the singular, undeniable source of good things.

God knows how your gift works and how you can use it most efficiently to benefit those around you. He doesn't leave you to figure out how to use your gift; instead, He makes sure you have access to His Spirit—the Helper, Teacher, and Counselor.

This is important because once you know where your gift comes from and who taught you how to use it, then it becomes impossible for you to take credit for anything beyond obedience. Your decisions are a vital part of the process, but the true driving force doesn't come from some personal courage. So instead of boasting, honor God for the good work He's doing in your life. Thank Him for a strength you don't possess on your own.

Do you know what your God-given gift is? If so, how have you shared it with others in a way that honors God?

BE THE MAN
WHO'S CONTINUALLY BEING REMADE

I am certain that God, who began the good work within you, will continue his work until it is finally finished on the day when Christ Jesus returns.

PHILIPPIANS 1:6 NLT

Lots of men excel at good intentions. They start projects and *almost* complete them. . .but then set them aside to do something else. Eventually, they have a dozen or more mostly finished jobs on the back burner. "I'll get around to it someday," they tell themselves.

There are remodeled rooms all over the world in which the work is 95 percent complete, but the lack of trim or new door hardware keeps it from perfection. In such cases, those few small steps to the finish line may never occur.

God is better than good intentions. When He starts the project of remaking men like us, no delays, back-ordered supplies, or diminished interest will force Him to stop—His work is over only when we're finished.

And that won't happen until Jesus comes back, so God stays pretty busy.

Gain strength from knowing you're more than an abandoned, half-finished project. You are a work in progress! And this progress isn't a weekend warrior event. Every day, God leads you in new directions, inspiring better choices with greater compassion. He can do for you what you can't do for yourself.

Now is not the time to give up. Now is the time to celebrate the "future you" with the God who finishes what He starts.

Do you live knowing that God isn't finished with your life? Why is that important?

BE THE MAN
WHO GAINS STRENGTH BY SERVING

If anyone speaks, they should do so as one who speaks the very words of God. If anyone serves, they should do so with the strength God provides, so that in all things God may be praised through Jesus Christ. To him be the glory and the power for ever and ever. Amen.

1 PETER 4:11 NIV

Your mouth says words you don't mean, utters promises you won't keep, and speaks phrases that offend. Speak "God words" instead. Your body language expresses discomfort, sends bad signals, and shows your disdain for serving others. Get "God strength" and serve. Don't speak words that only share your opinion—speak words that glorify God. You don't serve people; you work for the God who wants people to know He lives. That's why He asks you to serve Him by serving others.

Men who keep to themselves and refuse to serve grow weaker for their lack of involvement. Strength evaporates in the world of "I don't wanna." Unlike schoolhouse games, where everyone hopes to be picked first, some men see things they could do in God's name but hope for someone *else* to do it. They hope the assignments run out before their name is called. They might even devise a plausible excuse for turning a task down.

God will ask others to do what you will not, but it will always be your missed opportunity. Why champion a cause but choose something else instead? Why stress the importance of spreading the gospel when you sit blissfully ignorant of the person sitting next to you? Face it: the adventure of the Christian life is reduced when you place your willingness on "standby" mode.

A man of strength steps up, speaks, and serves.

Why do you think the act of speaking and serving is so important to God? What can you do today to make the concept personal?

BE THE MAN
WHO EXECUTES
GOD'S PLAN

I can of mine own self do nothing: as I hear, I judge: and my judgment is just; because I seek not mine own will, but the will of the Father which hath sent me.

JOHN 5:30 KJV

Jesus never strayed from the heart of God. He was no loose cannon. He did not go rogue. Jesus was revolutionary, but only compared to the sinfulness of man. Every single person violated at least one of His laws. No one was perfect; everyone was flawed. But here's the truly revolutionary part—Jesus' sacrifice satisfied the justice we deserved. . .and gave us forgiveness instead!

God had a plan, and Jesus executed the plan. God had a will, and Jesus had a willingness. If this hadn't been true, His forgiveness would be out of reach. Jesus sacrificed His human body to pay the sin debt of every human in history. He was the only one who could complete this impossible rescue mission.

The strength He showed, even in the mundane

moments of His life, proved that the same potential exists in you. He chose to be committed to God's plan—so can you. He obeyed God's direction—so can you. He did the hard things with God's help—so can you.

You haven't been left without an example—without a reassurance that following God is truly possible. You've not even been left with a reasonable doubt about God's love for you. God said you needed forgiveness, and Jesus agreed. . .then He made forgiveness possible.

Gain strength in God's rescue plan.

How does knowing you have an example
improve your strength while following God?
How can your response to God's plan alter
your willingness to do something?

BE THE MAN
WHO REMEMBERS
GOD'S FAITHFULNESS

The Lord will work out his plans for my life—for your faithful love, O Lord, endures forever. Don't abandon me, for you made me.

Psalm 138:8 nlt

Psalm 138:8 could be considered a nonessential prayer. God had already promised to never leave His people. The psalmist surely knew this, but it didn't change the fact that he sometimes felt he was on the verge of abandonment.

It's possible to doubt God's promises, even if you know all His other words have come true. You might pray the beginning part of today's verse—"The Lord will work out his plans for my life"—with the courage of a lion. . .and then follow up that bold statement by begging, "Oh, by the way, please don't leave me."

You might believe God was faithful in the past but wonder if it was a limited-time offer. You know God has answered your prayers, but maybe He's too busy this time. You ask for help, but you also wonder if you're pressing your luck.

Gain strength by knowing you can ask God. Even if He says no, your honest question will not bother Him or cause Him to turn away. His faithfulness lasts forever. It doesn't waver with inflation, political upheaval, or personal opinion.

You should never treat God with disrespect, but even if you do, this won't change His faithfulness to you. Remember: mankind's rebellion was why Jesus came to make things right between us and God. He didn't wait for humanity to achieve perfection—He knew that's not possible. However, Jesus' perfection makes up for it.

Today, follow the psalmist's example and remember that God is *always* present and faithful. He's here right now. And in that knowledge, gain new strength.

Where is God when you beg Him to never leave? Why is this important to remember?

BE THE MAN
WHO STANDS
AND RESISTS

*For we are not fighting against flesh-and-blood enemies,
but against evil rulers and authorities of the unseen world,
against mighty powers in this dark world, and against evil
spirits in the heavenly places.*

EPHESIANS 6:12 NLT

What do you think of when you picture yourself as a
soldier in God's army? Lots of gear and body armor?
Boot camp and early morning drills? A physical enemy?
A lifetime of veteran discounts?

None of these are entirely accurate. God's soldiers
come in all shapes, sizes, ages, and cultures. They may be
transferred and recommissioned, but they don't retire.
Our enemy isn't another person—it's an army of spiritual
powers.

This type of warfare can sound ominous, but that's
just what the enemy wants you to think. God's command
to His soldiers remains simple: stand and resist. If you
do this, the enemy will step away from the fight. When

you refuse to run, he eventually will.

You'll never gain strength by sitting and welcoming the enemy to a conversation. This is one of the easiest ways for the devil to disarm you and reduce your interest in following God's orders. He'll make it seem like he's a friend, but the moment you set your shield aside and take a moment to rest, he will accuse, condemn, and mock you for being a failure. Your strength as a soldier diminishes with each passing remark of the enemy.

So today, man of strength, stand—and resist.

Why does God say that our enemy is not human? How might that change your opinion of what to stand for—or against?

BE THE MAN
WHO REFUSES
TO BE UNHINGED

Those who hope in the LORD will renew their strength. They will soar on wings like eagles; they will run and not grow weary, they will walk and not be faint.

ISAIAH 40:31 NIV

Strength seems fickle sometimes. Some days, you may feel like you can take on the world, but then a single comment or situation unravels your confidence and leaves you unhinged.

Yet God.

Your belief in this one name will extend strength, add perspective, and inspire the perseverance needed to endure. God alone can infuse you with the strength it takes to face down circumstances that would otherwise leave you. . .unhinged.

Eagles soar and gazelles run, and they make it look easy. A trained athlete makes impossible feats seem effortless. They cross the finish line in a fraction of the time it'd take you on a good day. Just trying to match their time might leave you. . .unhinged.

You observe the success of people who follow God, and you wonder why your own life is any different. God suggests you stop looking at others to gauge your own progress. When you conclude that you don't measure up, it can leave you. . .unhinged.

Isaiah 40:31 gives a foolproof way to avoid this state of personal insecurity: trust. You don't soar, run, or walk because you're better than others; you do it because God has renewed your strength and made you "hinged" once more.

Does the term unhinged *make you uncomfortable? Why do you think it's so easy to compare your abilities with those of others?*

BE THE MAN
WHO KEEPS
FRIENDS CLOSE

The LORD is my strength and song, and he is become my salvation: he is my God, and I will prepare him an habitation; my father's God, and I will exalt him.

EXODUS 15:2 KJV

Once upon a time in the fictional world of Hollywood, there was a family that could understand what their dog meant just by listening to her bark. They listened to her vocal emissions and said something like "What is it, girl? You say Timmy's stuck in a well?" Maybe you have a dog like that—maybe you're certain its insistent barking means something more than a need to go outdoors.

A man in the western United States is thankful his dog showed that level of persistence. The human (unclear if his name was Timmy) tumbled down a steep mountain slope and injured himself. His best friend, seeing the problem right away, went looking for help. This dog wasn't much of a barker; he just did some impressive acrobatics that involved a fine display of jumping and spinning. But that urgent display was enough—help was on the way.

Sometimes, God sends you strength through a friend's persistent encouragement. This friend doesn't run away when you fall but gets help when you need it. This is the type of friend described in Exodus 15. But you don't have to meet the perfect person to find the perfect friend—God helps you. He knows the hurt you feel the deepest, and He stays with you and sends His Spirit to assist.

The worst predicament you'll ever face is no trouble for your Best Friend.

Who comes to mind when you think of your best friend? Why do you need God as a friend more than any other?

BE THE MAN
WHO LOOKS
BEYOND GUILT

Look to the LORD and his strength; seek his face always.

1 CHRONICLES 16:11 NIV

When you're off track and held together by the most fragile threads of guilt, you might avoid seeking God. And when people are vocal about rejecting God, ignoring Him may seem like a great way to avoid ridicule. It's easier to stay quiet, place some distance between yourself and God's help. . .and then conclude you've made a *very* big mistake.

When you follow this track, you're both denying yourself new strength and tossing existing strength to the wind. Your threads of guilt intertwine to form a tapestry of weakness. Its ugly style is noticed by all.

People often spend more time running away from God than toward His strength. Jonah was such a person. He wore his guilt and weakness better than most. He spent too much time showing God he had no intention of obeying. Instead of seeking God's face, he chased whatever wind would take him as far away from God's assignment as possible. But since Jonah would not chase God, God chased him. God knew Jonah needed time to think, so He sent a very large fish to find him. After three days inside the fish, Jonah finally agreed to replace his weakness with God's strength and trade his guilt for God's forgiveness.

When you have a chance, read the book of Jonah. It's not a long book, but it proves how worthless it is to reject God's free offer.

Today, God is willing to share His strength with you. Will you accept?

Why is it so easy to embrace personal guilt?
How willing are you to accept a strength
you'll never obtain on your own?

BE THE MAN
WHO'S A MODEL
FOR HIS KIDS

He giveth power to the faint; and to them that have no might he increaseth strength.

ISAIAH 40:29 KJV

If you have children (or might someday), know that they want to look up to you. They want to see you as a role model they can trust. What happens if you portray yourself as a man of strength. . .but never as a man who might get things wrong? What if they see your weakness but know you'll never admit it?

For most men, it sounds wrong to admit their weakness to their kids. They'd rather portray themselves as brave, courageous, and strong. But insecurity has a way of exposing the very lie it tries to hide. You can't *wish* strength into existence. You can't consume a dose of "instant strength" like some muscled sailor man who loves his spinach. Your kids know it, even when you won't admit it.

How do they know? Because they know themselves.

They struggle. They fight burning tears of anger. They sense that life is out of control.

So admit that you struggle too. Get real about the impact life has on you. You don't have to go into every little detail, but your children need to know that it's normal to feel hurt, scared, and confused when life is at its toughest.

What if your children never know your strength comes from God? What if all they see is you trying to pull yourself up by the proverbial bootstraps? What if your anger suggests you won't accept their compassion?

Let your kids know that it's okay to feel out of control—that this situation is exactly why they should ask God for help. That can be their response. Is it yours?

Do you try to let your children see your need for God's help? Why might it be a good idea to allow your children to hear you asking God for assistance?

BE THE MAN
WHO CAN STAND

The LORD gives his people strength.

PSALM 29:11 NLT

"When I run, I feel God's pleasure." Many people believe that the famous track star Eric Liddell actually said these words, but that isn't true: they came from a movie that portrays his life. Even so, Liddell likely would've agreed with them.

Liddell was a world-class athlete when he ran in the Paris Olympics in 1924. He chose not to run on the Lord's Day—and was disqualified for it. He'd already won in one category and placed third in another, but Liddell gave up the chance to snag a third trophy. Eventually, he left running altogether to become a missionary. Was his decision driven by strength or cowardice? Fear or freedom? A good moral compass or an error in judgment?

It was almost as if God were asking him, *Which do you trust more: Me or another shiny neck accessory?* Would this athlete be strong enough to say no to the call of the starting line, or would peer pressure set his feet to running once more? For Eric Liddell, it wasn't the strength to run that he needed—it was the strength to obey. God gave him that strength.

There will be times when you'll need the strength to stand, to fight off the overwhelming urge to collapse in defeat. You'll recognize this strength when you resist what you know is wrong in favor of a strength you're waiting to receive. The decisions you make in difficult situations will demonstrate where your strength comes from. It'll prove what you believe to be true about the God of strength.

Why is there no such thing as a break from obedience? How can obedience improve your strength?

BE THE MAN
WHO REJOICES
IN THE LORD

Nehemiah said, "Go and enjoy choice food and sweet drinks, and send some to those who have nothing prepared. This day is holy to our Lord. Do not grieve, for the joy of the LORD is your strength."

NEHEMIAH 8:10 NIV

The backstory to Nehemiah 8:10 is a thrilling adventure. After grieving the destruction of the walls in Jerusalem (which had been mostly abandoned nearly seven decades before, when God sent the people into exile), Nehemiah was sent to Jerusalem to rebuild. When he was finished, the people began to return. For many of them, this was a new experience—they'd not been born when their parents had been sent away.

Upon arriving in the city and hearing God's Word, the people were in a festive mood—boisterous, even. Yet the longer they listened, the quieter their cheering became. They were confronted with the decisions that had removed their families from the city, the sin the nation had embraced, and the judgment that had placed an exclamation point on their long rebellion.

The mood turned somber, and the celebration was nearly abandoned. The people seemed ready to go home and obsess over the sins of their fathers. That's when Nehemiah stepped in and reminded them that this was a time to honor the God who'd reestablished freedom, not to grieve an unchangeable past.

Nehemiah told these former captives that their grief would cause them to become weak, but the joy found in what God had done would infuse their hearts with new strength. And they'd need this strength as they brought the city, left to years of ruin, back to its former glory. Suddenly, the hearts of men, women, and children who were accustomed to the tragedy of ruin had been invited to new life.

What reminds you that your past is different from your future? How does this change your present?

BE THE MAN
WHO AVOIDS A
STRENGTH DEFICIT

My soul melteth for heaviness: strengthen thou me according unto thy word.

PSALM 119:28 KJV

Have you ever experienced a melted soul—the crushing feeling that all good things have come to an end? Your memories of good times fade, replaced by bitter regrets. Your heart is shattered, your mind is bruised, and it seems like your body is ready to self-destruct. This isn't an invitation to get depressed—it's just a relatable description of life's worst moments. Maybe you're even there right now.

Depression is a universal no-fun zone. It's what drives some people to make terrible long-term decisions that negatively affect everything.

If you weren't aware of a strengthening God, a melted soul could very well mean the end. But when you feel those emotions start rising, reread Psalm 119:28 and make it your prayer. You have a choice.

It's not foolish to admit you need help. Left to our

own devices, we'd *all* make the wrong choice. You have a strength deficit, and you can't fool yourself. You might even admit the fact. . .but still wallow in your weakness instead of seeking God's strength. But all this does is eliminate your willingness to try. Pity becomes your new best friend, but the more time you spend with him, the more you'll hate him.

Leave this place. Look for the "God space" that can change your perspective, drive weakness away, and infuse your melted soul with fresh and reviving strength.

Why does a little weakness, left unchallenged, always lead to more weakness? Why is pity detrimental to a melted heart?

BE THE MAN
WHO'S NOT AFRAID
OF DOUBT

[The man asked Jesus,] "Have mercy on us and help us, if you can."

MARK 9:22 NLT

Imagine a guy meeting Elvis Presley back in the day. This person doesn't know him, but he's heard about Elvis' special gift. So he tells Elvis, "Sing, if you can."

Now imagine someone telling Thomas Edison to invent something, "if you can." Roger Staubach to throw a touchdown pass, "if you can." Patrick Henry to stand up for freedom, "if you can."

We look at these questions and laugh. Of course Thomas Edison could invent, Roger Staubach could throw a ball, and Patrick Henry could stand for freedom.

Keep that in mind when you read the story about a man who came to Jesus and said, "Help us, *if you can.*"

This was the Son of God! Nothing was impossible for Him. He would heal the sick, raise the dead, feed thousands with a little bread and fish, and even rise from the dead. Whom did this guy think he was talking to?

But Jesus didn't use this moment to highlight His résumé; He didn't get upset, chew the man out, or refuse to help. Jesus had mercy on this man and his family. He helped even when this man expressed doubt.

This man's lack of belief did not diminish Jesus' strength, nor did it dismiss the man's need. Jesus didn't have to set the man straight about His power. He just. . .helped.

When you need a strength you can't find on your own, come to God—even if all you have to offer is one request and a lot of doubts. Believe what you can and allow God's strength to increase your trust.

Why is it okay to express doubt when you pray? What might you learn from the experience when God proves faithful?

BE THE MAN
WHO DOESN'T MIND
LOOKING FOOLISH

God chose the foolish things of the world to shame the wise;
God chose the weak things of the world to shame the strong.

1 CORINTHIANS 1:27 NIV

Some guys are brilliant and have multiple degrees, and some look like they could bench-press an SUV. Even if they don't announce it, the way they speak and conduct themselves can make other men feel insignificant.

If you are relying on your popularity or your ability to impress, you're in for a rude surprise: public opinion changes. God, however, uses a different metric. In the hands of God, weak people can become undeniable tools of strength and tenacity. Wisdom doesn't always come from a school, nor strength from a gym.

God takes what others consider deficits and uses them to make a huge impact in your world. He uses what some call foolish and weak to do things the smart and strong can only dream of accomplishing.

Maybe the reason for this lies behind the differences

between weak and strong, foolish and smart. Intelligence and muscles tend to build pride, which clouds a man's ability to recognize his need for God to work in his life.

To be clear, there's nothing wrong with being strong or smart. . .but neither of them will get you where God needs you to be.

Does the idea of being weak and foolish sound undesirable to you? In what ways can it be a good thing?

BE THE MAN
WHO INTERACTS
DIFFERENTLY WITH GOD

[Peter] took [the lame man] by the right hand, and lifted him up: and immediately his feet and ankle bones received strength.

ACTS 3:7 KJV

You are fragile. Your body can break, and so can your mind. Age has a way of cruelly reminding you of your younger days, when personal strength seemed to be in ready supply. Failure and weakness can sneak into your life, and you won't even realize they exist until you reach for your strength and discover there's not enough for the trouble at hand.

On your own, there's no way to escape the despair.

In Acts 3, Peter and John encountered a crippled beggar. . .and quickly perceived he wanted something much more than money. So they gave the man an unexpected prize: they "lifted him up: and immediately his feet and ankle bones received strength." Afterward, this man went into the temple with Peter and John and had his own worship service.

As you age, it's tempting to embrace bitterness and anger. But God's strength offers a better way. It doesn't just make you a nicer person—it keeps you fit for lifelong duty. A broken body might require you to perform your duty in a different way, but God never sets you aside. He won't ask you to do anything that He hasn't given you the strength to do. This may not be physical strength but an inner strength that's rooted in the goodness of God. Either way, it'll make a difference.

The strength God offers changes not only you but the way you interact with Him.

How can God's strength bring you to a place of worship? Are you using God's help to honor Him?

BE THE MAN
WHO SHARES
HIS STRENGTH

I long to visit you so I can bring you some spiritual gift that will help you grow strong in the Lord. When we get together, I want to encourage you in your faith, but I also want to be encouraged by yours.

ROMANS 1:11–12 NLT

Housewarming gifts may not be as popular today, but they were once a way to show friendship and hospitality—to congratulate them on their important decision.

Today, most people live by the motto "Let your presence be your gift." Consequently, gifts are no longer required or expected. But Romans 1 reminds us that the best housewarming gifts are the ones that come from *God*.

These gifts are spiritual in nature, and they come from the hand of Someone who recognizes their value. They include things like strength, hope, forgiveness, love, kindness, mercy, and compassion. These gifts are priceless.

When God gives you strength, take it with you. Every gift He shares is a gift you can share as well. Even if others refuse it, the importance of this gift can never be diminished. God gave it to you, so you can keep giving it and never run out.

God's strength can be passed along, and you have the opportunity to make that happen. Encourage and be encouraged—that's the cycle of sharing.

Are you intentional about sharing the strength God's given you? Why is this important in the Christian life?

BE THE MAN
WHO PROCLAIMS
FUTURE STRENGTH

Do not gloat over me, my enemy! Though I have fallen, I will rise. Though I sit in darkness, the LORD will be my light.

MICAH 7:8 NIV

Today's verse is the proclamation of an entire nation. God was about to place Israel in a time-out, and their enemies would no doubt find it amusing that they'd been so bad that God had to treat them like children. How weak and helpless Israel must've appeared! Of course, the enemy was right. On their own, the Israelites had been weak and ineffective. But God's goodness simply wouldn't allow them to stay in this weakened state. The people needed to understand that this was a corrective action designed to improve their strength. They would need to feel confident in following God once more.

Micah's proclamation was clear—the people had fumbled in darkness and fallen, not knowing where to go. But as bad as this proclamation seemed to be, it wasn't the end. Hope, assurance, and victory waited on the other side of their time-out. The people could say in unison that even though they had fallen, their story would end in victory. Despite the present abundance of darkness and despair, God Himself would be their light—their only source of rescue and clarity.

That's why strength could be found in the hearts of the fallen, hope in the minds of those living in darkness, and endurance in the souls who recognized God's plan. Through their new commitment to the God whom they'd once abandoned, they would begin their journey back to good health. He was waiting for their return—all they needed was His strength.

How long does God wait for the fallen to seek Him? Why is correction sometimes necessary to remind us of the source of true strength?

BE THE MAN
WHO IS AN OVERCOMER

Whatsoever is born of God overcometh the world: and this is the victory that overcometh the world, even our faith.

1 JOHN 5:4 KJV

Whenever you do something you thought you could never do—whether it's swimming, going to the dentist, or giving a speech—you are an overcomer. Everyone overcomes something. When you're very young, you might have a fear of the dark, spiders, or certain people. But when you beat back the challenge of coexisting with these things, you embrace the role of an overcomer.

Sometimes, overcoming comes naturally, like the process of growing up. But other times, you'll encounter things you can't overcome on your own. This might include trauma from childhood, ethnic prejudice, or memories of a violent encounter. The struggle can be debilitating—and even worse, no one else may understand. They might think it's silly, like a fear of the dark. But each tide of fear leaves you feeling overwhelmed and powerless—the furthest thing from an overcomer.

You start believing you'll never conquer this inexplicable fear. You come to hate this place, and you'd love nothing more than to toss this pain in the garbage bin.

First John 5:4 declares that it's faith in God alone that allows you to overcome the tough stuff. That's why God can wisely ask you to do what you think is impossible—to forgive those who hurt you, love those who hate you, and pray for those who fight against you. If God's commands can make *these* actions possible, there's *nothing* you can't overcome!

What's the most appealing thing about becoming an overcomer? How can you use God's Word to overcome?

BE THE MAN
WHO RECOGNIZES
DECEPTION

You belong to God, my dear children. You have already won a victory over those people, because the Spirit who lives in you is greater than the spirit who lives in the world. Those people belong to this world, so they speak from the world's viewpoint, and the world listens to them. But we belong to God, and those who know God listen to us. If they do not belong to God, they do not listen to us.

1 JOHN 4:4-6 NLT

Sometimes, leftovers are better than the freshly served meal. Why? Because time has allowed the flavors to seep into every morsel. It gets richer the more you come back.

The Bible can be the same way. Take a familiar verse like 1 John 4:4, for example: "You have already won a victory over those people." Yes, that's comforting. . .but have you ever asked yourself, "Who are *those people*"?

The first three verses of this chapter speak of people who shared popular spiritual philosophy without welcoming God into their thinking. These unwise preachers had a following, which made life difficult for Christians who understood that God's truth contradicted such guesswork. So whom did people believe? The men who learned from Jesus or the men who only accepted what they wanted to believe and then added their own teachings?

If some people won't listen to Jesus, they certainly won't listen to you. But their faulty reasoning is no match for God's strength, which makes even the best of human wisdom look foolish.

God 1—Deception 0.

Do you get upset when you hear people encouraging others to believe lies about God? How can you gain strength from knowing God has overcome faulty thinking?

BE THE MAN
WHO OVERCOMES THE WORLD

Who is it that overcomes the world? Only the one who believes that Jesus is the Son of God.

1 JOHN 5:5 NIV

There are lots of things you can overcome: faulty thinking, unproductive habits, addictions—you name it. Success in these struggles can improve your life and strengthen your relationships.

"The world," in 1 John 5:5, is presented as something to be overcome. But what exactly is "the world"? The earth itself? While God gave humanity the responsibility to "rule over" creation (Genesis 1:26 NIV), that's not what 1 John 5 is describing. So what is this "world" that John mentions? Who does the overcoming, and where do they get their strength?

Back in Genesis, God created a "very good" world (1:31 NIV). The only thing the first man and woman were told to avoid was the very thing that created our need to overcome: sin. Once sin arrived on earth, it never left.

We can't remove it, pay the price for it, or make it go away. But Jesus can.

Overcoming the world takes something bigger than our own personal effort. It takes an admittance of personal failure, a restoration of forgiveness, and an acceptance of rescue. When a man does these things, his faith in an overcoming God allows him to overcome "the world"—specifically, the sin that made this world such a sorry place.

Overcoming the world. . .what could be stronger than that?

What personal challenges do you want and need to overcome? How can the message of 1 John 5:5 encourage you in the struggle?

BE THE MAN
WHO'S A GOOD NEIGHBOR

Be not overcome of evil, but overcome evil with good.

ROMANS 12:21 KJV

God's strength can do what you can't. It can help when you won't and love when you'd rather not. God's strength welcomes the good choice—a kind word and a willingness to help. It opens closed doors, puts caution tape around your old stomping grounds, and lays out a welcome mat for others who don't know the source of your new strength.

Fred was a man whose approach to life displayed the fruits of God's strength. He was uniquely gifted in making both adults and children feel accepted. He encouraged people even when they didn't understand his motives. He loved people even when they made fun of him. He could've been overcome by evil, but Fred consistently chose to distribute good. And people noticed.

You might know this man as Fred Rogers (or perhaps "Mr. Rogers"). He was a pastor who was commissioned to share his faith through children's television. Many people still remember and celebrate him and his neighborhood—that's how different his life was.

It can be easy to trade love for a gavel—to become so bent on exacting justice that you forget all about forgiveness. Or you might do the opposite: forsake justice and not care enough to offer the other person help when it's needed the most.

Be a man who uses God's strength to make a difference.

Why might it seem intimidating to make good your natural response? What is one way you can choose good over the next seven days?

BE THE MAN
WHO PLEASES
HIS FATHER

Since we are surrounded by such a huge crowd of witnesses to the life of faith, let us strip off every weight that slows us down, especially the sin that so easily trips us up. And let us run with endurance the race God has set before us.

HEBREWS 12:1 NLT

If you watch enough movies about father-son relationships, you'll notice a common trope: dads are exceptionally busy. And because of their busy schedule, their seat is empty at sporting events, ballet recitals, and play performances. Their kids usually respond with dejection and frustration, to which the dads respond with a laundry list of excuses.

This is a relatable situation. Many men have disappointed their kids with unkept promises. Even if the situation is unavoidable, the sting remains long after the event was over. Even worse are the promises that some men never intend to keep. In these cases, a mere apology and a nice gift can never cover their failure.

Thankfully, there's a big difference between human fathers and Father God, the promise keeper. He not only shows up—He brings His own cheer squad! Every day is race day, and you never have to wonder if God is up there watching you run. He joyously pays attention as you use what you've learned from Him to run the race and bound over hurdles.

Your life is an endurance race, and God notices and rejoices when you persevere. So be a man of strength, endurance, and joy. Your momentum is growing.

Why do boys want their dads to be present for important moments? Why is it important to know God does this for you?

BE THE MAN
WHO PURSUES
STRENGTH IN TRUTH

"You will know the truth, and the truth will set you free."

JOHN 8:32 NIV

Do you live with God's impressive strength? You can.

It may not even seem like a strength at first. You may want to dismiss the idea as odd, maybe even a bit of insanity. But here's the scoop: you will grow stronger when you know and accept God's truth. How does that make you strong? It sets you *free.*

When you are free, you become more confident in your choices. Now, we're not discussing a permission to do whatever you want to do, whenever you want to do it. No—this freedom means you're no longer prevented from doing what God designed you to do. You become confident in following Him, listening to His whispered guidance, and then doing what you know is right. And you understand this because you have encountered truth, accepted it, believed it.

You become God's man of strength when you have

fewer questions about your path and greater trust in your guide. Your growing confidence may feel a bit like working for one employer for a long time. At some point, because you've been paying attention to how your boss wants things done, you just know what you need to do. You begin to understand why things are done the way they are. You trust the boss enough to do things just the way he asks.

Those things make a difference in your occupation. They also make a difference when you're pursuing God's truth. It leads to freedom—the freedom to be His representative among everyone you meet.

What do you think of the equation
Truth + Freedom = Strength? In what ways
is confidence important to improved strength?

BE THE MAN
WHO ALWAYS
CARRIES LIGHT

The light shines in the darkness, and the darkness can never extinguish it.

JOHN 1:5 NLT

Call it illumination, perspective, or even a front-row seat to God's work. You are welcome to a world of light that God makes available to you. You can use that light to gain a clearer picture of where God is working. . .and go there!

Here's the truth about light—as long as it exists, darkness can never be complete. Even a small amount of light displaces the surrounding darkness. When light shines in darkness, this light can prevent others from stumbling in the dark.

This is important for when you're tempted to leave your light behind when you go out in public. Doing so only achieves two negative outcomes: (1) it makes you confused about where to go next, and (2) it removes the incentive for anyone else to follow God's light.

This is why God's strength is hard to find among

those who refuse to name God as their source of strength. It's difficult to discover God's love among people who are always trying to hide His light. Concealing God's light can also make a man appear arrogant—it gives the impression that he doesn't think he needs help. While the people in darkness struggle to find their way, the last thing they need is someone who pretends the darkness doesn't exist.

God doesn't ask you to do anything He won't do, but neither does He ask you to do things He doesn't equip you to do. So when He asks you to carry His light into a spiritually dark world, it isn't to draw attention to you—it's to draw attention to the light giver.

When have you failed to take God's light with you? How did that go? How might God's light change the way you interact with others?

BE THE MAN
WHO ACCEPTS HELP

By grace are ye saved through faith; and that not of yourselves: it is the gift of God: not of works, lest any man should boast.

EPHESIANS 2:8-9 KJV

To be saved is to be rescued from a perilous situation. Flood victims may be plucked from a roof by a helicopter or pulled by rope from a raging river. Tornado victims are saved by search teams sorting through debris or simply neighbors checking on neighbors. The need for rescue is never diminished by how well you prepare or how much you hate asking for help.

Your spiritual life is no different. You can't boast about not needing God, because you'll *always* need God. You can't rescue yourself, and you can't buy His help. Why? It's a gift. You can either accept a gift or reject it, but you can't buy it. That would make it no longer a gift but a purchase. God's rescue could never boil down to an exchange between bank accounts. No one could afford it.

You are strengthened when you acknowledge that God

took you from a path of destruction and applied healing, light, and love to make you something more.

Rejecting God's rescue won't make you stronger—it'll leave you as vulnerable as the man on a roof during a flood shouting at his rescuers, "Don't bother; I can make it!"

Don't tell God you just need to try a few more ideas on your own—embrace His rescue today.

Why is it a bad idea to believe you can rescue yourself? How has being humble enough to ask God for help changed you?

BE THE MAN
WHO LOCKS FEAR OUT

Even when I walk through the darkest valley, I will not be afraid, for you are close beside me. Your rod and your staff protect and comfort me.

PSALM 23:4 NLT

If God wants you to be strong, that means He doesn't want you to be afraid. Fear tells strength there's no vacancy—it steals into each room and redecorates the place. Inside, it's dark and foreboding. Danger lurks in every shadow, making it impossible to find the exit.

When God leads you, however, He gives you the power to deny fear a place to stay. When He's beside and before you, your soul becomes a place of protection and reassurance.

Confidence doesn't mix well with anxiety. Courage is weakened by worry. Yet too often, it feels like anxiety and worry are all we've got. A man might try to shrug them off or boast of how well he's handling it all. But inside, when no one else is around, he feels like a scared boy dreading his next nightmare.

If a man were honest about his true inner state, he'd probably use words like *cowardice*, *frailty*, *distrust*, *uncertainty*, *humiliation*, and *timidity*. None are fair companions. No one wants them around, yet everyone knows who they are. No one pursues them, yet everyone spends time listening to them.

God wants you to spend time with Him instead— it's the only way to lock the door when anxiety comes knocking.

Why is it important to keep your life fear-free? What is one way you can replace fear with faith today?

BE THE MAN
WHO LEARNS
FROM SUFFERING

The God of all grace, who called you to his eternal glory in Christ, after you have suffered a little while, will himself restore you and make you strong, firm and steadfast.

1 PETER 5:10 NIV

Everyone suffers. Some just don't talk about it much. Even Jesus suffered. And God the Father suffered when He watched Jesus die on a cross. God suffers when people around the world break His laws. He suffers when you suffer.

Simply put, suffering is the act of experiencing something you'd rather not experience. For some, it may be a traffic jam when time is short. For others, it may be bullying. It can be the loss of a job, a bad health report, or a relationship issue.

When it comes to enduring suffering, we could all take a lesson from plants. Some can only endure the scorching summer months if they've weathered the fall and winter and come through *hardened*. This agricultural term means to intentionally remove young plants from the protection of a greenhouse so that they can adapt to the wild temperature swings in the great outdoors. Without this hardening, a plant may flourish in the greenhouse but die very quickly when placed outside.

Protection feels great. . .but too much of it can make you weak. God's Word makes it clear that trouble comes to all men—but God uses it to inspire patience and perseverance. Trouble teaches men to follow hard after a very good God.

A man of strength sees sorrow as an arduous college course, where God teaches His pupils how to weather this messy and disheartening world.

Have you ever learned more about God through suffering? How did His strength help you move beyond the trials?

BE THE MAN
WHO CHOOSES
MEEKNESS

A truly wise person uses few words; a person with understanding is even-tempered.

PROVERBS 17:27 NLT

A man of strength is also meek. This can confuse people, especially those who define *meek* as "timid, shy, and somewhat fearful." But Jesus had another definition in mind: "humble, gentle, and kind." None of those three words describe weakness.

Think of it this way—meek people don't brag about what they can do; they just do it. They're not rough in dealing with people, but they are strong enough to be patient. They're not bullies; instead, they're compassionate toward those who have struggles of their own.

A man who embraces true meekness is exceptionally strong because he strives to be the man God made him to be. He chooses silence over arguments—understanding over anger. He seeks to understand the situation before drawing a conclusion, so he's rarely the first to react. And when he does react, he does so to de-escalate. He's also extremely trustworthy, never hesitating to allow God to work in his life.

Needless to say, being meek isn't easy. Is it any wonder that Jesus said in Matthew 5:5 (NLT), "God blesses those who are humble [meek], for they will inherit the whole earth"?

Do these thoughts challenge the way you view meekness? Why is it important to find the perfect balance between strength and meekness?

BE THE MAN
WHO LIVES IN
GOD'S YOKE

[Jesus said,] "Take my yoke upon you and learn from me, for I am gentle and humble in heart, and you will find rest for your souls."

MATTHEW 11:29 NIV

Strength isn't a commodity that can be bought or sold. It's not a self-help program that assures success in three easy steps. It's not even something you are born with. Strength is a gift—someone has to give it. And this someone is God, the strength giver. Without Him, strength doesn't exist.

God can give you lessons in strength development. He wants you to watch Him work, personally observing His goodness, and then to join Him. Refusing to go where He's working will leave you uncertain about His strength. But participating—working right alongside Him—will teach you how to do things the way He wants.

Being meek means being humble, gentle, and kind. . .and God is your greatest example. It's His meekness that demonstrates His great strength. Reread Matthew 11:29 for a clearer picture of how God wants you to learn as you work with Him in His strength.

The "yoke" described in today's verse is the linking of God's heart, mind, and will with your own. This helps you move in God's direction. It enables you to see what He sees when He's at work in the world.

A man of strength lives in God's yoke.

What have you learned while working alongside God? Do you find it odd to think of God as meek?

BE THE MAN
WHO FEELS VALUED

I give each of you this warning: Don't think you are better than you really are. Be honest in your evaluation of yourselves, measuring yourselves by the faith God has given us.

ROMANS 12:3 NLT

You've probably heard that God is strong, while you are weak. This is true. And it's also true that recognizing your weakness invites God's strength to assist you. On the other hand, pretending to be strong only proves that you're weak.

God wants your personal evaluation to be accurate. He wants you to recognize who you are—no better, no worse. You are a sinner saved by grace. You are broken but being remade. You are a formerly lost slave who's been made an heir to God's kingdom.

Yet many men love playing the comparison game. Eager to present themselves as better than their peers, they miss the honest evaluation God asks for.

Admitting you are weak shouldn't make you feel like a victim. Instead, God's empowering strength, love, and forgiveness should make you feel like a victor who is part of an amazing partnership—one that nobody deserves but any can enjoy.

Comparing yourself to other people will poison your soul, spill from your lips, and hijack your heart. It's a game in which nobody wins. All it does is cloud your perception of how much God values you.

Don't strive to be better than anyone else—simply ask God to help you be the best you possible.

Do you find it easy to compare yourself to others? Why is this a poor evaluation method?

BE THE MAN
WHO FOLLOWS A
DIFFERENT LIST

Therefore, as God's chosen people, holy and dearly loved, clothe yourselves with compassion, kindness, humility, gentleness and patience.

COLOSSIANS 3:12 NIV

There are a lot of words that people use to describe men. They include *arrogant*, *proud*, *powerful*, *tough*, and *aggressive*.

What a different world it would be if men presented themselves the way God wants! His Word offers a different list of words that describe a man who uses His strength. This list includes *compassion*, *kindness*, *humility*, *gentleness*, and *patience*.

Despite popular misconception, true strength isn't the ability to manipulate circumstances to conform to your plans. Instead, God's strength values personal relationships over personal agendas.

Christians are set aside for use by God. He loves and cherishes them more than any human can. And when a man like you clothes himself in God's attributes, the resulting impact in his culture will be more profound than a massive wave of arrogant, proud, powerful, tough, and aggressive men.

To be clear, God's not denying the benefits that come with physical strength. He's simply saying that true strength is more than you can find in the gym. And if you can't adjust your understanding of strength to fit God's definition, then you're actually settling for spiritual weakness. You're relying on your own power, thus missing out on a greater power you can never possess on your own.

If this challenges your thinking about strong men, then this may be just what God intended for you to read today.

Why might it be hard to accept God's description of a man? What's one tangible way you can incorporate some of the items on God's list in your choices today?

BE THE MAN
WHO THINKS ABOUT
THE FUTURE

We are citizens of heaven, where the Lord Jesus Christ lives.
And we are eagerly waiting for him to return as our Savior.

PHILIPPIANS 3:20 NLT

There's a compelling reason to accept God's strength—He gave you the body you have, and He'll give you a new one someday. Your future body will be designed to last forever. That's why God doesn't emphasize keeping your current body in shape. True, He does say your body is where He lives—but that's only to highlight the strength He brings to your relationship with Him.

When you start contrasting your temporary earthly existence to eternity, then this time and place suddenly seem pretty small. Why spend so much time trying to impress people when you won't be able to do it for long?

For Christians, life on this big blue marble is but a blip. Earth is merely the place where we choose what happens after our last breath.

God never intended for you to live forever in the "here

and now," especially since a "then and there" awaits. While you're here, you're given an extraordinary opportunity to seek wisdom and discover what's really important. So your best course of action depends on what you should look forward to the most.

Your strength-giving God provides the strength for the body you have right now. . .and for the eternal one that's waiting for you.

How does knowing there's more beyond this life alter your view of the strength God offers? Do you think of this place as temporary housing or a permanent residence?

BE THE MAN
WHO BELIEVES
BEYOND THE IDEA

For the Kingdom of God is not just a lot of talk; it is living by God's power.

1 CORINTHIANS 4:20 NLT

God isn't just an idea, concept, or fairy tale. Don't let anyone tell you otherwise, even if that person attempts to make your faith seem foolish.

God's Word is the foundation of all truth, and it teaches that He has always been and always will be. And since God created everything—and since He remains your only hope for rescue—why would you ever devalue or mock His name?

But even if you do, His response to you will be love; His gift, forgiveness. His kindness is the best antidote to rebellion. His power is greater than the jeers of the disbelieving. His love is mightier than those who want Him to leave. His open arms are more powerful than your ability to run away.

If you believe that God is a concept, idea, or fairy tale,

then you've missed the point—this so-called fairy tale *created* you. His kingdom coexists with your rebellion, but He will work tirelessly to chip away the defenses of your heart.

In the grand scheme of life, rebellion against God makes you weak. Changing your address to God's kingdom, however, brings strength. If rebellion is uncertainty and suspicion, then strength is assurance and growing faith.

Why do some see rebellion as strength?
Why will this never be true? Have
you invited rebellion to leave?

BE THE MAN
WHO KNOCKS OFF
THE PRETENDING

God is our refuge and strength, an ever-present help in trouble.

PSALM 46:1 NIV

What would happen if you were able to handle every challenge and carry every burden without God's help? Would God mean more or less to you? If you knew you could solve every problem, wouldn't God start taking a back seat in your life?

The practical reason for weakness is that it proves how essential God is. He has always been able to do what you can't, to go where you won't, to love when you don't.

When God shows up and saves the day, it removes all doubt about who's really in charge. But this shouldn't lead you to self-pity; instead, it should be a profound reminder of your connection to an amazing God who loves you and wants to guide you through life's challenges.

Weakness is simply a reminder that everything you lack is readily available through God. The benefit of this arrangement is that you'll always have what you need because God replaces your weakness with His strong plan of action.

Somehow, weakness has become taboo—something to avoid at all costs. But this attitude flies in the face of the human experience. If you refuse to admit this truth, you're deceiving yourself. Instead of accepting God's help, you keep pretending that you're better than everyone else. This minimizes the needs of others and inhibits any growth in your friendship with God.

Is it hard for you to admit that you need God's help? Why is there such a stigma attached to this admission?

BE THE MAN
WHO IDENTIFIES
WITH JESUS

The Word was made flesh, and dwelt among us, (and we beheld his glory, the glory as of the only begotten of the Father,) full of grace and truth.

JOHN 1:14 KJV

There was a time when God's Son, Jesus, had a human body. He was still God, but His body would end in destruction. Jesus could be hurt, injured, and drained of health. He had the strength of God. . .coexisting with a weak body.

Jesus was beaten, bruised, and hung from a cross. People abused Him, pierced Him with thorns, and pulled the hair from His beard. He was subjected to more physical pain than most will ever experience.

If the Son of God experienced weakness in a human body—if He had to ask God to help Him—then why wouldn't you think it's the same with you?

When you refuse to ask God for help, you're saying you are superior to Jesus. That may not be your intention, but it's the message that's conveyed every time you turn down God's essential help.

Jesus recognized that the human body had limitations. He knew that sometimes He just needed to talk to God about life's unrelenting waves of struggle.

All human bodies, including yours, have a shelf life. Your physical strength will decrease over time, but the strength God offers will last until the end of this life and throughout the eternal life that comes next.

So why settle for physical strength? There's more to life than this.

Does thinking about Jesus' struggles impact your willingness to ask God for strength? Why or why not?

BE THE MAN
WHO EMBRACES
SPECIAL SKILLS

Put on all of God's armor so that you will be able to stand firm against all strategies of the devil.

EPHESIANS 6:11 NLT

If you're asked in a job interview to share your personal strengths, you'll probably reply with something that's relevant to your desired position. If it's a desk job, you probably won't mention how great you are with disc golf, video games, or chain saws. (And you definitely don't want to bring up the "Most Likely to Take a Nap" award your family gave you.)

But there's one set of skills that is useful for *every* task: the "armor of God" that's described in Ephesians 6. If you learn to use this armor effectively, you'll be remembered for believing in the truth, valuing the peace found in God's Word over the chaos found elsewhere, relying on faith to improve your responses and cut out distractions, and trusting God's salvation as the source of all these skills.

The more you learn from God, the greater your inner

strength becomes. The armor of God makes you not only a better person but a better employee, a better friend, and a better husband. It places you shoulder to shoulder with God, who stands with you when you face the enemy's lies. And when you're tempted to brag, it encourages you to remember who did all the rescuing.

Do you strive to apply the armor of God to every area of your life? How does this skill set add strength to life?

BE THE MAN
WHO BELIEVES
WITHOUT FEAR

Jesus told [Jairus], "Don't be afraid; just believe."

MARK 5:36 NIV

Jairus was a religious leader who believed in God, followed Him, and told other people about Him. But the religious leaders of his day didn't equate Jesus with God. That's why they stood tall and proud about their connection to God. . .while totally missing God's Truth who stood before them day after day.

When his daughter became very sick, Jairus acted like a daddy. Hating to see his daughter so ill, he did something highly illogical—he sought Jesus to see if He could help. But just as he found Jesus, he received word that his little girl had died. Put yourself in his shoes for a second. All sounds blur into an odd, silent roar. Tears well up, ready to burst from their gates—hindered only by the watching eyes all around. You're a loose cannon, standing face-to-face with God.

That's when Jesus gave a command that broke the

sound barrier, drove Jairus' tears back, and called forth a strength he didn't think was possible: "Don't be afraid; just believe."

Strength leaves when fear is allowed to stay. Weakness renews its contract when you fail to believe. But you can't believe in just anything—you must believe in a good God with a good plan. He can calm your darkest fears, but when you don't believe He can do it, then fear only tightens its grip on your heart.

Jesus gave this advice to Jairus. . .and that day, his daughter rose back to life.

When are you most likely to pray for God's help? Why is belief in God's strength always the right call on a bad day?

BE THE MAN
WHO'S NOT INTIMIDATED

Don't be intimidated in any way by your enemies. This will be a sign to them that they are going to be destroyed, but that you are going to be saved, even by God himself.

PHILIPPIANS 1:28 NLT

Struggle is inevitable. And when it comes, it will prove beyond a shadow of a doubt that you have weaknesses. But whether you moan and bewail your situation or take practical steps toward victory is up to you.

Your enemy is God's enemy, and his primary goal is to prevent you from trusting. . .and thereby keep you weak. He's managed to keep some people in this sorry state for decades. But you can be different.

When you stand strong in the strength only God can supply, God's enemy has lost already. Even the devil's mightiest attacks are powerless in the face of God's strength.

You may have heard that we're supposed to resist the devil, not trash-talk him. But the Bible clearly teaches that this isn't a conversation—it's a confrontation. As a soldier in God's army, you are to resist Satan's attack while God deals with Satan himself. God doesn't need your help to do that.

Your soul—the part of you that goes on after death—remains untouchable by the enemy when you accept God's rescue. Even when Satan does his worst, God has already given His best. . .so the outcome of this struggle should never be in doubt.

When is the best time to remind yourself that Satan loses in the end? How can this knowledge change the way you face him? Why is this sometimes so hard?

BE THE MAN
WHO FINDS STRENGTH
IN OBEDIENCE

"Then you will have success if you are careful to observe the decrees and laws that the LORD gave Moses for Israel. Be strong and courageous. Do not be afraid or discouraged."

1 CHRONICLES 22:13 NIV

King David, who was currently on the throne, gave instruction to his son Solomon, who'd soon take his place.

It wasn't strategy that David spoke of. It wasn't the cleaning schedule. It wasn't the intense demands Solomon might face. Instead, David knew that Solomon's relationship with God would make or break his leadership.

David knew how easy it was for a king's brain to grow discouraged and fearful after a full day of complicated decisions. Such a mindset leads to a place of weakness and vulnerability. No king wants that. So David told his son the key to his success: obeying God and gripping the strength and courage that He offered.

Solomon would have to trust when it was hard to trust, obey when God's commands contradicted his plans, and stay courageous when the storm clouds of fear started to gather. Is it any wonder that Solomon asked God for the wisdom to lead the people?

You need strength. That isn't a question—it's a fact. The two most famous kings of Israel admitted this, identified the source of their strength, and prioritized it in their administration. They knew that unless they passionately pursued a strong and strength-sharing God, their power was really no power at all.

Do you strive to make your pursuit of strength a generational pursuit? How might you pass along what you're learning to someone in your family?

BE THE MAN
WHO PURSUES
TRUE LIFE

*When I am afraid, I will put my trust in you. I praise God
for what he has promised. I trust in God, so why should I be
afraid? What can mere mortals do to me?*

PSALM 56:3-4 NLT

King David made some bold statements in Psalm 56:3–4.
He said that faith beats fear. He said it was worth honoring God for the faithful promises He's made. But he also
said something that may seem like a death wish—he said
that not even plans designed to harm him would change
his fear-busting faith.

If he was beaten? No fear. If he was tortured? He
would trust. Even if he was killed? He would be with
God. This king saw no downside to the worst that could
happen to him.

The same is true for you. The worst any other human
can do is take your life. . .but God *gives* life. If your earthly
body wears out or dies, it only means your eternal life
with Him starts sooner than expected.

King David wasn't being cavalier about suffering. He just fully understood that because God would take care of him forever, even the worst-case scenarios weren't worth his attention. It's not that he was asking for death—he just realized that *true* life can't be found by living in a constant state of fear.

No one had the power to take God away from the king or to touch the eternity that awaited him. How's that for reassuring news?

How can King David's conclusion encourage you when you're struggling the most? What about in even the most mundane situations?

BE THE MAN
WHO KNOWS
UNMEASURABLE LOVE

So that Christ may dwell in your hearts through faith. And I pray that you, being rooted and established in love, may have power, together with all the Lord's holy people, to grasp how wide and long and high and deep is the love of Christ, and to know this love that surpasses knowledge—that you may be filled to the measure of all the fullness of God.

EPHESIANS 3:17–19 NIV

The road to God's strength isn't paved with peace and prosperity—it's a rugged ride headlong into the wind of God's great adventure. You'll face opposition, you'll become weary, and you'll start wondering if the troubles are worth it after all.

But you'll also witness something that far outweighs these difficulties. You'll get to experience a love that can't be measured or understood. You'll get to learn that God remains with you, even when others run away.

If life were perpetually easy, what use would you have for God's strength? If work came without effort, how would you ever overcome the temptation of weariness? If there were no bad days, why would God ever need to encourage you?

There's nothing bigger than God, stronger than His love, or richer than His mercy. Because trouble is a promise, so too is your access to the strength that helps you overcome this trouble.

Gain strength from knowing there's no place you can go where God's love won't follow you. There's nothing you can do that will cause God to turn His love away. Never mistake trouble for a lack of love—consider it an opportunity for God to show you how much He cares.

When was the last time you sought strength in the fact that God loves you? How can God's love strengthen your spiritual spine?

BE THE MAN
WHO BEGINS
WITH WEAKNESS

I had to feed you with milk, not with solid food, because you weren't ready for anything stronger. And you still aren't ready.

1 CORINTHIANS 3:2 NLT

Like it or not, weakness is a great launching pad for strength. But staying weak isn't what God has in mind. This would be like trying to prevent babies from growing up by treating them the same forever. In both our physical and spiritual lives, there's a growth pattern that changes our abilities, desires, and techniques.

Some men *choose* weakness over strength. Maybe the idea of strength overwhelms them or seems too good to be true. Maybe they know what God wants but refuse to act. Maybe they're afraid they'll miss the milk after they give solid spiritual food a try.

It's hard to grow strong when you're doing everything you can to stay weak. Admitting your weakness isn't enough—you must have the desire to change. This change doesn't depend on your abilities but on your willingness to be strengthened by God.

Once you see the futility of doing what you've always done and somehow expecting a different result—once you stop arguing with God or defending your lack of obedience—God will start making you a new creation.

You have a choice: Will you stay weak. . .or find new strength?

Have you ever refused God's strength?
What would be the outcome of
continuing to do things your way?

BE THE MAN
WHO SIMPLY
STANDS FIRM

So, if you think you are standing firm, be careful that you don't fall!

1 Corinthians 10:12 niv

Peter was a living example of the warning in today's verse. As soon as he thought he was standing firm, he fell. . .hard. No doubt thinking there was no other disciple as dedicated or brave as he was, he made brash promises and bold statements. He was a proverbial foam hand—Jesus' number one guy. But Jesus didn't buy it. And He certainly didn't celebrate it.

Peter was incapable of giving a fair and accurate self-evaluation. He must have thought he was top of the class and more reliable than most. Yet unlike Jesus, when Peter made a promise, he consistently broke it. His self-proclaimed strength was exposed as a profound blind spot of weakness.

If this would happen to you, would you be able to sleep at night? Would you ask yourself why you had such trouble holding your tongue? Would you wonder why you were motivated to make promises you couldn't keep? Yes, you might have been trying to impress the Son of God, but maybe you overlooked the most obvious truth—it's not about what you *think* you can do but what God *absolutely* can do.

Peter refused to admit weakness, even after blowing it over and over again. He still thought he could master his impulsiveness without God's help.

When you stand firm, remember who is holding you up. You don't need to buy a T-shirt that says you are standing firm. You don't need to wave to the crowds. Pride has no place in standing firm. You stand with help.

Are you ever tempted to boast about your ability to stand strong? How might this boasting turn people away from seeking God?

BE THE MAN
WHO PRAYS FOR
WEAK MEN

Epaphras, a member of your own fellowship and a servant of Christ Jesus, sends you his greetings. He always prays earnestly for you, asking God to make you strong and perfect, fully confident that you are following the whole will of God.

COLOSSIANS 4:12 NLT

What if you had the opportunity to petition the God of the universe to step into someone's life and give that person a taste of divine strength?

Seeking strength doesn't have to be solely for yourself. Plenty of people are wallowing in the muddy pit of weakness right now, believing their life will never be anything more. If you can't convince them on your own to give God a try, ask God to pursue them and introduce them to real strength.

You know weak men who live in the cycle of addiction, pornography, and failed relationships. They want to change, but they dismiss the possibility as a mere fairy tale. *It'd be nice to have this kind of strength*, they think. *If only it were real.* It may be so far from their experience that they start viewing the strength they see in other people's lives as weakness.

Everyone's been there. It might happen when someone intentionally rejects or walks away from God. Or it could be a knockout after a twelve-round bout with pride. It could even stem from the fear of walking away from weakness.

Many people need to discover that the strength they need is the strength God offers. Pray for these people today.

When was the last time you prayed for God to strengthen someone you know? How might praying that kind of prayer today make an impact you've so far been unable to make?

BE THE MAN
WHO'S NOT AFRAID
OF STRENGTH

The disciples were in trouble far away from land, for a strong wind had risen, and they were fighting heavy waves.

MATTHEW 14:24 NLT

Nature's strength—the kind found in tornadoes, hurricanes, earthquakes, tsunamis, and blizzards—can be impressive but frightening.

The disciples were in a boat in the middle of the lake when they witnessed the full extent of this power firsthand. On their own, they had little chance of battling the storm and reaching shore.

The closest thing to the disciples' terror that most of us feel happens as we're sitting in a storm shelter or waiting out a hailstorm in our car. We hear the earth rumbling, the dishes clattering. Fear creeps in as we imagine what the world will look like once the storm passes.

In Matthew 14, Jesus proved that even nature's strength is subject to God's. This storm wasn't over yet, but when Jesus spoke, the raging chaos stopped—no questions or delays.

The strength of a storm is a perfect image of chaos—of a frightening power far out of our control. But God has no problem controlling it. And since God has the strength to stop a storm, why shouldn't you believe He can calm the storm that rages in you? In fact, He can do even better—He can *give* you the strength to do the impossible.

Which type of strength seems the most overwhelming to you? How can it help to know that even this power is subject to God?

BE THE MAN
WHO ACCEPTS
SUSTAINED STRENGTH

And the child grew and became strong in spirit; and he lived in the wilderness until he appeared publicly to Israel.

LUKE 1:80 NIV

John the Baptist was born with a purpose. He was a voice in the wilderness—a human megaphone that shouted, "Hey! Have you noticed Jesus?" And in doing so, John pointed others toward the same strength he himself possessed.

John was more than willing to look foolish and even weak to those who didn't understand. He was given a purpose—and then the strength—to do something God created him to do. John didn't care if people made fun of him or thought him strange. God's strength sustained this preacher, so when the time came to introduce Jesus to the world, John didn't hesitate. And once God's Son actually arrived, he began to quickly step back. Jesus had a much bigger job to do, and John was determined that he wouldn't stand in the way.

This man grew strong in spirit because he kept close to God. He chose obedience over notoriety—and at the right time, he set the stage for God's main attraction. Jesus' message of salvation then grew in the void left behind by a vanishing wilderness preacher named John.

God gave you a purpose, and He can also give you every ounce of strength you'll need to fulfill it. But this requires your full cooperation—a willingness to step down when God wants another to rise. Do you have that kind of strength?

Does public opinion ever sway your willingness to use the unique gift God gave you? How does God's strength enhance your purpose?

BE THE MAN
WHO SEES STRENGTH

Therefore, brothers and sisters, in all our distress and persecution we were encouraged about you because of your faith.

1 THESSALONIANS 3:7 NIV

Your level of spiritual strength isn't just about you. It impacts your family, friends, neighbors, coworkers, clients, and even strangers. When people are in distress, they can be encouraged by your display of a strength that can only come from God. It can make onlookers consider the possibility that weakness can be overcome.

Perhaps that's one reason why God tells Christians to associate with Christians. None of us are perfect, but the more time you spend with God and His believers, the more likely you are to witness moments of strength. On the contrary, if you never observe strength, renewal, and growth in the lives of those around you, it might be hard to believe God's promise of strength.

Whether a man is the encourager or the encouraged will depend on where he's found in the weakness/strength cycle. The church is full of broken, hurting people. . .but healing can be found in God and His Son, Jesus. Only He can inject new life into a body, mind, and soul defined by weakness.

Often, it takes a moment of desperation to make us reach out for God's strength. But God is not some miserly being who makes it hard for you to find His strength. You can look around at any time and witness the truth—there's strength in the body of Christ! Rejoice because this strength can also be yours.

Do you think it's important for you to see God's strength lived out in the lives of people around you? Why should you want to live life with other believers?

BE THE MAN
WHO KNOWS EVERYTHING'S GONNA BE ALRIGHT

He shall be like a tree planted by the rivers of water, that bringeth forth his fruit in his season; his leaf also shall not wither; and whatsoever he doeth shall prosper.

PSALM 1:3 KJV

Some people seem to be born for greatness. You might have someone in mind right now. Such people make great choices and stand up for what's right at seemingly the perfect time. They are great examples who may even seem larger than life.

But these same people often don't think of themselves as worthy of any accolades. During their moment of "greatness," they might've been scared senseless and simply wanted to hide. But bravery isn't the absence of fear—bravery simply tells fear who's boss.

Each of the Bible's heroes lived in that place where fear meets faith—a place in which God's voice whispered in their ears, "Everything is going to be alright." At this intersection, you get to decide: Will you be the man

God needs you to be, or will you shrink back and wonder if you'll ever have this chance again?

Psalm 1:3 describes the man who chooses the first option as a tree nourished by the perpetual flow of a river. His roots pull deep draughts of God's goodness, causing him to bear fruit that others see. Spiritual sap runs rich inside his limbs and inner rings, growing long-lasting leaves that provide shade to those around him.

Be the man who invites others to discover the shade, refreshment, and fertile soil of God's strength.

How does your strength depend on your placement? Why must faith displace fear before strength can show up?

BE THE MAN
WHO KEEPS
"GOD COMPANY"

Because of Christ and our faith in him, we can now come boldly and confidently into God's presence.

EPHESIANS 3:12 NLT

A man of strength is bold, confident, and brave. He is nourished by Someone greater than himself. This man finds it easy to come to God and speak his mind. He lays his concerns on the table. His heart is an open book. His dreams are transparent.

Does that describe you?

God invites this kind of conversation, and He'll strengthen you to begin it today. Talk—He's listening. Listen—He's got things to share.

Today's verse explains how this connection is possible. You can come to God with a boldness that exists "because of Christ and [your] faith in him." It isn't because you are naturally bold enough to bring your trouble to the Creator of life. You're not strong enough to stand in His presence and feel anything but overwhelmed, unworthy, and undone. But because of Christ, you have that strength. You've tapped into the nourishment that causes godly growth.

A man of strength refuses to treat God as a temporary solution. God isn't just reliable when you feel stumped. A friendship with Him shouldn't be like calling 911—He wants to be in contact with you at all times. Why would you settle for less?

How did Jesus' work make it possible for you to pray? How does your prayer life grow stronger by following Jesus?

BE THE MAN
WHO SPENDS TIME
WITH GOD'S SPIRIT

They were all filled with the Holy Spirit and spoke the word of God boldly.

God uses four terms to describe His Spirit: Counselor, Guide, Helper, and Companion. Doesn't that sound like the friend you've always needed?

It's easy to overlook the Holy Spirit. The Bible is full of stories about Jesus and God the Father but far less about His Spirit. And the few that do exist are easy to pass over because we don't quite know what to do with them.

But God's four terms give us some great information about His Spirit. Because He's a counselor, He'll have some great advice. Because He's a guide, He'll offer great direction. Because He's a helper, He won't leave you when you need Him. Because He's a companion, He'll share the journey with you.

The last six words of Acts 4:31 take this understanding even further: all this counseling, guiding, helping, and friendship should lead to improved strength. . .which in turn keeps you walking with God and sharing His message with others.

When you allow God's Spirit to help you, you shouldn't be surprised when you obtain an unnatural boldness. Peter and John, the subjects of today's verse, had been taken captive, interrogated, and ultimately released. But instead of growing quiet and finding a place to hide, they experienced the boldness that came from God. When they made room for God's Spirit, God's Spirit made room for strength. Strength was just what they needed. So do you.

Do you make full use of the strength God's Spirit gives? How can you make it a priority to keep close to God's Spirit?

BE THE MAN
WHO RESPONDS
IMMEDIATELY

"I publicly proclaim bold promises. I do not whisper obscurities in some dark corner. I would not have told the people of Israel to seek me if I could not be found. I, the LORD, speak only what is true and declare only what is right."

ISAIAH 45:19 NLT

Every human has quirks. One person, for instance, may have a violently emotional response to a remark others would see as innocent. The mind of such people may seem like a confusing labyrinth. What you see isn't always what you get.

Not so with God. If He makes a promise, He keeps it. If He says something is true, it's always true. If He gives a road map, there's no need to guess where this road leads. He's always right. No exceptions.

There is strength in God's consistency. Why? It eliminates the need for hesitancy. If He can be trusted completely, then you don't need to weigh the risks of following Him. For instance, when God said that you shouldn't lie, you shouldn't start wondering, "Hmm. Is that *always* true?" If you do, your chances of lying increase. This is true for any of God's laws: the more time you take to believe them, the weaker you'll become.

A man of strength saves time by immediately going where God sends him. Once you remove your hesitation, you'll begin to see time saved, trust extended, and hope realized.

Have you ever spent time pondering what God wants—even when you knew the answer? How can decreasing your obedience "reaction time" make you stronger?

BE THE MAN
WHO DOESN'T CARE
WHO NOTICES

The fear of the Lord is the instruction of wisdom; and before honour is humility.

PROVERBS 15:33 KJV

Humility describes those who live without arrogance. They don't force people to pay attention to them. They don't have to be first. They don't chase publicity. So how does this relate to strength? Because God's strength is amplified in those who are humble.

A humble man won't tell you he's humble. He will simply show up with a strength that is greater than himself, whether you applaud or not.

Such men are wise because they learn from God. They are humble because they know God is greater than their weakness. God can use them because they are happy to let the credit fall to Him.

If there were a humility hall of fame, you'd probably find biblical men like Daniel, Joseph, Moses, and Job on the wall. But no such hall exists. Why? Because that would defeat the purpose of humility!

Humility recognizes the strength it takes to simply be awesome. . .without ever wishing for anyone to view you as awesome. You know that whatever awesome deeds you do stem from God, who doesn't need to brag.

A man of strength doesn't need a publicist to send out a press release on how amazing he is. What he does need is the conviction that only God is worth following 100 percent of the time—even when no one's watching.

How does God use humility to make you strong? Why is humility so hard to choose?

BE THE MAN
WHO IS VERY BOLD

If the old way, which has been replaced, was glorious, how much more glorious is the new, which remains forever! Since this new way gives us such confidence, we can be very bold.

2 CORINTHIANS 3:11–12 NLT

From the beginning, God loved mankind. He created a garden and met the first man and woman's every need. He spoke to them and spent time with them. . .yet they broke His only rule. Even though the promised penalty was eventual death, God worked with humans. But still, they turned on each other, killed each other, lied to each other, and sinned against God.

But even then, God still loved mankind, so He sent His Son, Jesus, to do something entirely new. Jesus would pay their penalty—death—one time for everyone. No longer would mankind be separated from a loving God. Now, the same kind of friendship He planned for the first man and woman—one that involved communication, teaching, and companionship—was made available for us all.

Knowing the vast scope of God's love should give you the strength and confidence to approach Him. Because of Jesus' permanent one-time payment for sin, God will never stop being available to you.

Be bold. Be strong. Be confident. The God who made it possible to come close will enable you to stay close. This new way, brought by the life gift of Jesus, means you'll have immediate access to God—always.

Why is complete access to God important?
Why does this new system offer more
strength than the old system?

BE THE MAN
WHO IS NOT ASHAMED

I eagerly expect and hope that I will in no way be ashamed, but will have sufficient courage so that now as always Christ will be exalted in my body, whether by life or by death.

PHILIPPIANS 1:20 NIV

In pretty much any battle scar–showing contest, Paul would win. He'd been shipwrecked, bitten by a snake, beaten, wrongly imprisoned, and betrayed by fellow workers.

But this great apostle hadn't always been an apostle. His career path did not lead to Jesus—Jesus' path led to Paul. And after that meeting (sometimes simply called "the Damascus Road Experience"—see Acts 9), Paul's life became more challenging.

Many in the church—remembering his believer-persecuting, Christ-hating past—didn't accept him. So instead of being a pharisaical enforcer, Paul became an outcast to both former Pharisees and those who followed Jesus. He didn't seem to fit. So God sent him away from what he knew to tell complete strangers about Jesus.

He would need to take a second job (making and repairing tents) to make ends meet. He would meet with resistance. He would feel the cold, hard stone of a dungeon prison.

Who chooses that kind of life? One who knows how little this temporary trouble matters in light of eternity with the faithful God. This scarred man knew that as long as Jesus was amplified in his choices, it didn't matter if he were killed. His courage proved to everyone he encountered that he was not ashamed of Jesus.

How often do you base your behavior on others' opinions? Why is it important to make decisions based on Paul's principles in Philippians 1:20?

BE THE MAN
WHO REJECTS FEAR

*One thing have I desired of the LORD, that will I seek after;
that I may dwell in the house of the LORD all the days of my
life, to behold the beauty of the LORD, and to enquire in his
temple.*

PSALM 27:4 KJV

King David understood that life was unfair. He knew that
people often seek to destroy what they fear. . .which often
includes parts of God's plan. Their bad choices stem from
a fear of God. This isn't a reverential fear—it's terror at
the thought of standing in the presence of love.

Psalm 27 relates a time when the future king encountered countless roadblocks. Some suggest the psalm is
about Doeg the Edomite, who'd hated David so much
that he killed eighty-five priests because one of them had
shown kindness to this soon-to-be king.

If this is the incident Psalm 27 is about, then these
words show David's strength of spirit that transcends fear:
"Though an host should encamp against me, my heart
shall not fear: though war should rise against me, in this

will I be confident" (Psalm 27:3 KJV).

In other words, David was saying that even if it took years—even if he never saw it happen personally—God would win against his foes. They could rise against him all they wanted, but they could never defeat God.

David, a battle-weary man in dire circumstances, had every logical reason to be scared. . .but he still turned to the strength only God can provide.

Have you ever been really tempted to give up? What kind of courage can you take from Psalm 27 in order to face your impossibilities?

BE THE MAN
WHO WALKS WITH ASSURANCE

They are confident and fearless and can face their foes triumphantly.

PSALM 112:8 NLT

Bad news is simply a half-told story—but it's the news in the largest font. Bad headlines grab the eye, and tragic endings capture the heart. Any good in the middle gets squeezed out of memory, replaced by all the bad bits. . .which then get passed down from generation to generation.

Many men are barraged with the bad news of betrayal, job loss, health issues, relationship stress, conflicts, and gossip. Most see injustice in these issues, so they either look for the chance to leave the scene or offer the person who's suffering some magical three-step plan that can solve every woe. Neither response is helpful.

God knows that the sin lodged in the heart of mankind will hurt you, but He also knows how to take this hurt and somehow make it useful—either to you or anyone around you.

Your struggle is indisputably real—real enough to take your breath away and steal your strength. Yet God keeps supplying the oxygen you need and the help you can't find on your own. He invites you to trust, even when rage is striving to find a voice.

When you understand that trouble (and all its nasty cohorts) is a temporary guest, then you can see your predicament with new eyes. Trouble has come before, and it left. It will come again, but it'll never be the end.

Why is it so hard to wait for good outcomes? When was the last time your story transformed from bad to good?

BE THE MAN
WHO FINDS STRENGTH
IN WAITING

If we hope for what we do not yet have, we wait for it patiently.

ROMANS 8:25 NIV

Patience is a strength that most want but few are willing to learn. Why? Because you have to wait for it! It doesn't come in a package in the "Virtues" aisle. It must be learned.

Patience is a word that conjures up ideas of endurance and perseverance. . .which both ultimately lead to strength. Getting patience means willingly attending a master class in struggle. It means not only experiencing the struggle but taking notes through the pain. Then you can apply this knowledge to your future decisions. It also means waiting is easier, since you now know all struggles come to an end.

When you don't have clarity—when answers are hard to come by—you're faced with a choice: become frustrated or become patient. Give up or endure. Throw your hands in the air or persevere. Sometimes, this choice is a split-second decision, in which you hardly have the time to think of the consequences. You might give up without realizing what a disaster that will cause.

That's why becoming a man of strength is so important: it'll make you comfortable with waiting—for both physical things and spiritual. You don't have the best life yet, but being patient means you're certain there's a better day to come.

Don't give up.

Why is waiting so hard for most men?
Has growing in patience improved
your trust in God? How?

BE THE MAN
WHO PARTICIPATES
IN GOD'S STORY

You are a letter from Christ showing the result of our ministry among you. This "letter" is written not with pen and ink, but with the Spirit of the living God. It is carved not on tablets of stone, but on human hearts. We are confident of all this because of our great trust in God through Christ.

2 CORINTHIANS 3:3–4 NLT

The greatest story you'll ever write will be in the lives of people you love and help. The good things that happen in the lives of these people show that your life was useful in strengthening someone who would have otherwise remained weak. The apostle Paul knew, wrote, and lived this truth.

On his missionary trips, Paul discovered that when God's Spirit led him to those who struggled, their story became part of his story. He met so many people and learned to love them deeply. He recognized that God was writing a story bigger than his own. This divine story was not only important but transformative.

By widening your sphere of influence, you gain confidence because you're no longer alone. God is working in you and others with the goal of bringing His children together to do a work that's greater than the sum of its parts.

A man of strength combines personal humility with the knowledge that he's part of God's bigger story. Serve with others, share in their story, and discover a bond among the faithful and forgiven.

Is it difficult for you to include others in your schedule? How can confidence in a shared goal provide a strength that you'd otherwise forfeit?

BE THE MAN
WHO LIVES ASSURED

God also bound himself with an oath, so that those who received the promise could be perfectly sure that he would never change his mind.

HEBREWS 6:17 NLT

The idea of being "perfectly sure" is impressive. It leaves no room for doubt and results in a growing faith. It implies a friendship that transforms worry and blocks anxiety. It's an invitation to witness a miraculous change. Assurance is just one more aspect of strength—and it doesn't come from you.

God made a promise to you, and He won't (and can't) change His mind. His love for you isn't based on your deeds, and it's never up for annual review.

How different the world would be if Christians truly internalized God's promise. If we were all perfectly sure that God's promises will come true. Gone would be the second-guessing, the late-night wondering, and our petty comparison games. We'd live without doubt, walk with no fear, and honor God with gratitude.

God's promises are many. Not only can He make you a new creation—He *will*. Not only did He start your story—He'll *finish* it. Not only did He give you life—He's made it *abundant*. His generosity is legendary. His grace is more than enough. His mercies are delivered daily.

A man of strength smiles with joy, lives with purpose, and presses on without hesitation. He celebrates good news and realizes that bad news isn't the final word. He believes the best about God and knows the worst in mankind can be transformed. He knows he's flawed, but he celebrates forgiveness.

These are just some of the things about which a man of strength is perfectly sure.

How does assurance of God's goodness translate into improved spiritual strength? Why is it hard to be perfectly assured? Is something preventing you from being certain about God?

BE THE MAN
WHO ESCAPES
THE STENCH

So God has given both his promise and his oath. These two things are unchangeable because it is impossible for God to lie. Therefore, we who have fled to him for refuge can have great confidence as we hold to the hope that lies before us.

HEBREWS 6:18 NLT

Imagine a world filled with uncertainty. Wait. . .you don't have to imagine that—you live in it every day. In this cesspool of uncertainty, the assurance you should celebrate doesn't seem to have room to grow.

But you don't have to live in the stench of this place. You don't have to exist in self-imposed exile. You don't have to fear every noise. God is both your refuge and your strength. Following Him provides all the reasons you need to back away from uncertainty, loneliness, and fear. Run to Him, leaving behind your trepidation. And never go back.

You've been given new life in the midst of old struggles. God's Word can replace the world's "spiritual junk food," causing you to look and act more like the God who brought you new life.

It might be tempting to stand tall and work things out on your own. But all that brings is self-inflicted loneliness. You'll have no one to help, no one to walk with you, and no one with whom to cooperate.

A man of strength will accept help and friendship. He doesn't exist to amass trophies, take home ribbons, and share stories of why he never needed God.

God has a future for you, so when you keep refusing His help, you're simply wasting time.

Have you ever tried to "go it alone" without God's help? What does it take to trigger your willingness to ask God for help? Why?

BE THE MAN
WHO UNDERSTANDS
ANCHORS AND CURTAINS

This hope is a strong and trustworthy anchor for our souls.
It leads us through the curtain into God's inner sanctuary.

Hebrews 6:19 NLT

Most people don't know much about anchors. Sure, we all know that anchors are designed to keep boats in place. But did you know there are numerous types of anchors? Yes, these handy devices come in types like Danforth, Fluke, Fisherman, Grapnel, Delta, Plows, Bruce, Bügel, Bulwagga, Spade, and Rocna.

There's even a difference between temporary and permanent anchors. The first can hold you in place for a while, but it might come loose, causing a noticeable drift. A permanent anchor, however, is designed to securely keep your ship in place.

But despite their differences, all these anchors have one thing in common—they're heavy. You wouldn't want an anchor made from paper!

There's another word picture in today's verse: curtains.

They are designed to be decorative, but they can also be designed to provide separation.

Okay, now back to the verse. The author of Hebrews says that your hope in God is like a permanent soul anchor. He won't let go, even when life's storms try to drive you off course. And this same hope that keeps you from drifting also welcomes you into God's presence. There is no more curtain. The No Trespassing sign has been removed, and a welcome mat has been put in its place.

A man of strength understands the value of God's anchor and the freedom in bypassing the curtain that once kept us from God. This hope comes from a perfect trust in a God who wants to spend time with you.

Does thinking of hope as an anchor inspire confidence in God? How can the idea of a removed curtain between you and God make you bold?

BE THE MAN
WHO APPROACHES GOD

This is the confidence we have in approaching God: that if we ask anything according to his will, he hears us.

1 JOHN 5:14 NIV

Let's take some time to focus on two words in today's verse: *approaching God.* In order to come near God, you have to believe that He exists, that He can be found, and that He wants to be near you.

Approaching God carries with it the idea of walking with God. You aren't running away or making fun of Him. You see Him as a worthy companion, friend, and walking partner.

By approaching Him, you are proclaiming that you're not afraid of this God who continually expresses love for you. It means you know where to go for answers, whom you can trust with your secrets, and what kind of relationship you want with the God who made you.

Approaching God involves being confident that He wants the best for your life. When you want the same thing, it pleases Him greatly. The strength you'll find in a friendship with God isn't transferable. . .but it is shareable. Your words and actions should cause someone else to want to approach God too. They might want to walk with Him, learn not to be afraid of Him, and embrace a new strength that frees them from a life of bad decisions.

You can be this man of strength. You can walk with God as a friend. You can find Him and share Him. So why not start today?

Do you find it hard to be confident when praying to God? How can approaching God bring an undeniable freedom to your friendship with Him?

BE THE MAN
WHO KNOWS THE SOURCE
OF CONFIDENCE

"The hopes of the godless evaporate. Their confidence hangs by a thread. They are leaning on a spider's web. They cling to their home for security, but it won't last. They try to hold it tight, but it will not endure."

JOB 8:13-15 NLT

Bildad was a wise man as well as a friend to a very rich man named Job. When the latter fell on hard times, the former used his wisdom to make seemingly practical conclusions. In other circumstances, Bildad's statement might have been enshrined as a fresh proverb. Many may have admired the words that flowed from his tongue. But because Bildad left empathy behind, what was otherwise a sound bit of wisdom became a blunt object that Bildad used to accuse Job of wrongdoing.

If you read the first chapter of Job, you'll discover that God's adversary had wanted to harm Job because he was certain God was unfairly protecting him. Job was innocent. Bildad, however, found it impossible to believe that. So this man who called himself Job's friend started kicking him while he was down. He essentially told Job that he had no reason to hope, that his confidence was fleeting, and that his riches would dissolve.

His words, while true for those who are actually godless, didn't bear the mark of a true friend. Bildad spoke without learning the backstory.

Don't let confidence come from what you know. . .but rather from whom you know. Love others, walk with them, and trust that God is working in their lives in ways you can't understand. You won't have to know their backstory to walk with them in the presence of your confidence-giving God.

How is confidence in God different from self-confidence? Have you ever allowed the second kind of confidence to replace the first?

BE THE MAN
WHO'S UNDER
THE INFLUENCE

The wise fear the LORD and shun evil, but a fool is hotheaded and yet feels secure.

PROVERBS 14:16 NIV

When you hear someone say an individual is "under the influence," nothing good usually comes to mind. To be under the influence suggests that a man is making very out-of-character (and usually very poor) decisions. Certain substances can induce this altered frame of mind, causing the guy to forget his own choices.

But did you know there are other "influences" that have the same effect?

You can be under the influence of bad advice and make similar poor choices. You could be under the influence of various forms of media, and it might alter how you view the world. You can even be under the influence of an untrue view of yourself, which will cause you to act in ways that don't reflect an accurate assessment of your character or purpose. This is especially obvious with pride, which can wrongly convince you that you're better than most or even cause you to rejoice in the suffering of others.

God wants you to be under the influence of His Word and His plan for your life. He wants you to reject self-assurance—and the harmful choices that often accompany it—for the certainty that He provides.

A man of strength stands in awe of God and resists evil. So today, embrace the confidence that comes solely from His hand. Accept God's strength and stand firmly under His influence.

Has self-confidence ever left you under the wrong influence? How can you change what influences you?

BE THE MAN
WHO TAKES THE
COURSE CORRECTION

The LORD's justice will dwell in the desert, his righteousness live in the fertile field. The fruit of that righteousness will be peace; its effect will be quietness and confidence forever. My people will live in peaceful dwelling places, in secure homes, in undisturbed places of rest.

ISAIAH 32:16–18 NIV

Isaiah seems like a book of doom mixed equally with gloom, with a liberal dash of despair for bad measure. This book tells the story of a people who rejected God and ignored His warnings. Maybe they thought He would never actually correct their behavior. After all, they'd been living in the wild embrace of sin for a very long time. They probably felt they were getting away with it. They might have felt God was too weak to mount a challenge to their lawbreaking ways.

They were wrong.

When the promised exile happened, it probably looked like disorganized chaos. . .but it was a promised alteration that would eventually lead them to newly discovered obedience.

God reinstated the high bar of righteousness for a people who had long forgotten what it looked like. He brought justice to facilitate His course correction. But then came His great and profound promise—peace, quietness, and confidence. Soon, this out-of-control crowd would finally obey. And when that happened, they would have security and rest. A national sigh of spiritual relief was just ahead.

What God wants to give us is exactly what we should want. It's certainly what we need. A man of strength is wise enough to trade chaos for peace, restlessness for rest, and uncertainty for confidence.

Do you need a course correction in your friendship with God? Are you willing to make that happen? How might you begin today?

BE THE MAN
WHO CHOOSES
FIRM STEPS

[God] lifted me out of the slimy pit, out of the mud and mire;
he set my feet on a rock and gave me a firm place to stand.

PSALM 40:2 NIV

We've all experienced setbacks that have left us sitting in a filthy pit of despair, wondering how we'll ever get out of this mess. We live on the fringes of this pit every day. One false move, and we're stuck and in need of help. But Psalm 40:2 offers some great news: we have a flashlight! Every day, we can access the wisdom of God's Word so that we can confidently know where to step.

Sometimes, spiritual failure is the most effective way to learn wisdom. But this route is never mandatory or even advisable. Intentionally breaking God's law to gain a better testimony should never be your goal.

You'll never gain God's strength by disregarding His guidance or walking with the wrong company. When you refuse strength that only God can give, you're declaring that you have every intention of remaining weak. Does that sound like a good admission to you?

You can—and should—be a man of strength. You can be weak all by yourself, but strength is a gift that's sourced in God. Allow Him to release your feet from the "sin mud" that keeps you a prisoner to bad choices.

Then. . .watch your step!

Where have your spiritual feet led you lately? How often do you let God know you want to be strong?

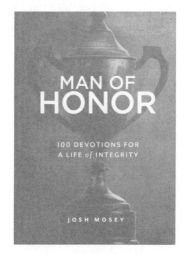